ATHENA'S DISGUISES

ATHENA'S DISGUISES

MENTORS IN EVERYDAY LIFE

Susan Ford Wiltshire

Westminster John Knox Press
Louisville, Kentucky

Scripture quotations, unless otherwise noted, are from the New Revised Standard Version of the Bible, copyright © 1989 by the Division of Christian Education of the National Council of the Churches of Christ in the U.S.A., and are used by permission. All rights reserved.

Grateful acknowledgment is made to SCM Press for permission to reprint from Dietrich Bonhoeffer, "The Friend" in *Letters and Papers from Prison*, The Enlarged Edition, SCM Press copyright © 1971, pp. 388ff.

Odyssey quotations are from the translation of Robert Fagles, 1996. Line numbers differ from the Greek text and from other translations.

Poems in the text, unless otherwise indicated, are the author's.

Book design by Jennifer K. Cox

First Edition
Published by Westminster John Knox Press
Louisville, Kentucky

This book is printed on acid-free paper that meets the American National Standards Institute Z39.48 standard. ∞

PRINTED IN THE UNITED STATES OF AMERICA
00 01 02 03 04 05 06 07 — 10 9 8 7 6 5 4 3 2

Library of Congress Cataloging-in-Publication Data
Wiltshire, Susan Ford, 1941–
    Athena's disguises : mentors in everyday life / Susan Ford
Wiltshire. — 1st ed.
        p.   cm.
    Includes index.
    ISBN 0-664-22101-7 (alk. paper)
    1. Mentoring in literature.   2. Literature—History and criticism.
I. Title.
PN56.M48W55   1998   98-7532
809'.93352—dc21

for MLB
first to stand by

CONTENTS

Mentor took the floor,
Odysseus' friend-in-arms to whom the king,
sailing off to Troy, committed his household,
ordering one and all to obey the old man
and he would keep things steadfast and secure.

Odyssey 2.250–54

PROLOGUE

The story that follows is about mentors, those companions for the journey who give us the courage to be who we are. The pathways and purposes they point out are not first of all their own but those they sense in us. Sometimes such persons are familiar friends, sometimes mere bystanders who know us hardly at all. When these individuals serve as mentors, however, their presence strangely transforms us. Their gifts, which we may recognize only after the fact, change our lives. The story I tell here was long in the learning, because until I was an adult I thought I had no mentors at all.

When I was growing up, I wanted to be a preacher. My reasons were not bad. I admired some of the ministers I knew, I liked people, I had a leaning toward performance, and I assumed that folks ought to be encouraged to be as good as possible. Being a minister seemed to me to be about the most worthwhile work anyone could do.

I wanted to be a preacher, but actually becoming one never once crossed my mind. Ministers were men, and I was a girl. Teachers were women, so of course I would be a teacher. (Only later would I discover that teachers were women but professors were men.) That was the way the world was made. It was a given, plain and simple. To think otherwise would have seemed as strange as a flock of colorful songbirds to one who previously had seen only sparrows.

Sparrows were, in fact, about the only birds I did see as a child in the Texas Panhandle in the forties and fifties. Except for a stray mulberry tree on the way from our home in Lubbock to our farm farther north in Deaf Smith County, the only trees I saw had been planted during the Depression by federally funded civilian workers or watered carefully in yards or windbreaks. I was sixteen years old before I laid eyes on a significant body of water. Arriving at night on a trip to Galveston, I heard the roar of the Gulf of Mexico before I saw it. The sound seemed uncanny.

This dry Panhandle land was a pitiless creditor to wheat farmers such as my father who planted their crops far beyond the reach of irrigation. Spring after spring, I agonized as the small green shoots of wheat withered and died. Fall after fall, I was amazed as my father went back to plant again. My parents were survivors of the Dust Bowl, so they knew the lot they had chosen. On Black Sunday, April 14, 1935, they were driving to Amarillo from their home in tiny Vega, the epicenter of the decade-long drought, when the sky turned so black with dust at noontime that they could not see their hands in front of their faces. Some thought the world was coming to an end. Nothing grew anywhere. Even milk cows had to be shot. Crows built their nests from barbed wire.

Such was the geography encoded in my consciousness and probably in my genes. I have a hunch that the fierce discipline of that hard land also shaped the realm of men who moved upon its surface. I can only tell you, however, the part of the story I saw firsthand for myself.

The third of four children, I was the only daughter among three brothers. That status was and still is privileged in many ways. Growing up, however, I was acutely aware that my brothers were living the important and interesting lives. They were all active in Boy Scouts. They went on long camping, hunting, and fishing trips. They took shop courses in junior high school instead of home economics. They participated in team sports. My two older brothers attended college at Texas A&M (as did our father), at that time still an all-male school with mandatory participation in the corps of cadets. All three of my brothers served in the military. Their worlds were closed to me.

I once heard a famous actress tell student performers in a master class that anything they would ever need for a play, they had already experienced by the age of thirteen. By that age I had in hand much of what I needed for living a life. I had a strong feel for the ways I had been formed by place, race, work, and religion—perhaps even an incipient understanding of these factors in fashioning a life. I had developed a strong interior life and many ways of coping.

I set out to discern the things that I could do and concentrated relentlessly on doing them as well as possible. My Methodist piety contributed its sometimes endearing and often precarious side: I felt obligated to achieve not only a self but a "be ye therefore perfect" self.

When I recall these years, I still feel an immense sense of isolation. Although raised by loving and caring parents, I felt alone, as if I were inventing myself. Perhaps most children do. In my case, the isolation was reinforced by my place in my family, by gender, and by social codes as implacable as the West Texas wind. If instead of wanting to be a preacher I had been drawn to a vocation in medicine, law, business, engineering, science, or politics, I would have fared no better in the matter of mentors. I did not know the term *mentor* then, but I would have seen that there was nobody ahead of me in any of those professions who could give me reason to think I could enter them myself. What I mean to say is, because I saw no women doing these things, these things clearly could not be done by me.

In time (because of a story to be recounted later) I decided I wanted to teach on the university level. All the way through graduate school and early into my teaching career, I still thought I had to invent myself because I had no one to point the way. Also, I still thought that only men could be mentors. In my case, if I had had mentors they would have been men, because I never had a female professor through four years of college and four years of graduate school.

My isolation proved to be empowering at first, then dangerous, and finally was redeemed by a story for which I had been waiting a very long time.

The story I needed, it turned out, had been there for me all the time, at least since I first heard about it from a classmate in the second grade at Roscoe Wilson Elementary School. It had been there also in my teaching for some years when, in my thirties, I read it one day as if for the first time. Perhaps we truly listen to stories only when we are ready to hear them at the level of our need. Here was a story far older than my own, older even than most in western culture, that revealed to me how many mentors I had.

The story was Homer's epic poem, the *Odyssey*. In the *Odyssey*, the goddess Athena assumes many roles as helpful companion for the hero Odysseus, his wife Penelope, and their son Telemachus. She is their advisor and guide at critical moments in their various journeys. She always fills this role, however, in disguise. Her disguises include those of male and female characters, young and old, friends and strangers. Athena's most frequent disguise is that of an old family friend named Mentor, Odysseus's former companion-in-arms. It was an important moment in my life when I finally came to see that the first mentor was a woman after all.

Equipped with this story, I began to see mentors all around. My narrow, limited understanding of mentors seemed to have diminished a life that in fact had always been rich with helpful companions. I was able to revisit and thus revise my past, as any good story helps us to do, for now I recognized how many mentors had accompanied my life all along.

1

THE WAYS
OF ATHENA

*And down Athena swept from Olympus' craggy peaks and lit on
Ithaca, standing tall at Odysseus' gates, the threshold of his court.
Gripping her bronze spear, she looked for all the world like a
stranger now, like Mentes, lord of the Taphians.*

Odyssey *1.119–23*

When Athena swoops down from Mount Olympus early in Homer's *Odyssey*, she is headed to Ithaca to help mortals. Her intervention is timely, because the leading characters in the epic are all in trouble. They feel alone and abandoned. They desperately need both guidance and companionship for the journeys each must take.

In order to help mortals, the goddess Athena arrives at Odysseus's palace disguised as a mortal. In her first appearance she comes as Mentes, a visiting ship captain who claims friendship with Odysseus but is a stranger to those presently in Ithaca. Soon she will reappear as Mentor, the old family

friend and trusted advisor whom Odysseus appointed to look after his household when he left home to fight the Trojan War.

In the course of the *Odyssey*, Athena—sometimes called
Pallas or Pallas Athena—serves as a helpful companion in
half a dozen or more human forms, all of them very much like
people we too encounter every day. This apparent familiarity
is one of the reasons the *Odyssey* continues to engage and delight modern readers. We see ourselves and those we know in
these characters. In this, one of the first texts of western literature, Athena helps those who need her in so many guises that
we who read it begin to recognize how many people in our
own lives have helped point the way for us.

About This Book

This book is not about how to be a mentor or how to go
about getting one. It is not "how to" anything. Rather, it suggests new ways of discerning the mentors already around us. It
encourages new openness to the companions in our lives
whose gifts we are receiving already.

What I explore here may be called the classical model of
mentoring, as contrasted with an instrumental model in
which someone ahead of us either signs up for the task or is
designated by others to help us get ahead in the business at
hand. The instrumental model can be and often is beneficial,
and I readily concede its usefulness. Later I will discuss examples of the instrumental model.

Mentoring in the classical sense, however, has to do with
discernment of choices rather than with self-advancement in
choices already made. It has to do with the company we keep,
some of it quite unexpected and perhaps short-lived. It has to
do with risk and change as we continue to grow. It has to do
finally with a strange assurance that we are not alone on the
road, that we are somehow "steadfast and secure."

Each of the seven chapters that follow centers on an appearance of Athena in the *Odyssey* in one of her different roles. These chapters portray seven categories of individuals who may serve as mentors for our lives: longtime friends of the family, relatives (including siblings), children (not necessarily our own), artists of all kinds, bystanders or passersby (people we hardly know), friends, and peacemakers in our communities.

While using the *Odyssey* as a starting point, I elaborate each story with examples taken both from my own experience and from that of people and books I know. This reflection on the *Odyssey* and mentoring is therefore not a scholarly book in the traditional sense. I sometimes smile to remember, nonetheless, that *scholarly* comes from the Greek word for leisure, and I am grateful to have had the leisure in my life to learn the old stories, live many new ones, and tell about some of them now.

In the second portion of this book I leave the *Odyssey* and turn to more general questions, some of them thorny, about the matter of mentors. What dangers might attend mentoring relationships? What about hierarchy and the exercise of authority? Can a superior—a teacher or a boss or a supervisor—be a mentor at the same time? What problems might arise from being someone's protégé? Can a community be a mentor? If so, what does that say about the uniqueness of individuals?

Gentler concerns in these later chapters include the conditions that foster mentoring. One of the most important is hospitality to strangers, but hospitality in the ancient rather than the modern sense of hosting merely one's friends. Both the Greeks and Hebrews believed that openness to strangers was a divinely-ordained obligation because the visitors might be gods themselves or otherwise heaven-sent. The other critical issue around mentoring is that it takes time, sometimes large amounts of time, to be available to others. In these later sections, I refer also to stories of mentoring from other traditions, including Vergil in Dante's *Divine Comedy*, Moses in the Hebrew Bible, Jesus on the road to Emmaus, and Krishna in the *Bhagavad Gita*.

Throughout the book there will be talk of gods and of God. With the polytheistic Greeks it is easy to be casual about the divinities because the Greeks themselves so often seemed to be. The monotheistic traditions, however, invite greater reticence. It is the reticence of Orthodox Jews who refuse to write the name of God because of the presumptuousness it infers, as if God could be defined by human beings. It is the reticence of Dietrich Bonhoeffer in a Nazi prison who said that he was more comfortable naming God to nonbelievers than to believers. Casual or reticent, gods and God enter into our stories.

In the conclusion, I explore the kinds of perspectives on living that might result from gratitude for the gifts we receive from the mentors around us.

For now, however, since the *Odyssey* is the founding document of mentoring and since episodes from the poem provide the organizing structure of this book, a brief review of the setting will serve as a reminder of the larger context of the epic.

The Setting of the Odyssey

Odysseus never wanted to go to war. Because of a pledge to support his fellow Greek king Menelaus if anything happened to the latter's beautiful wife Helen, Odysseus was unable to dodge the recruiters who came for him after the Trojan prince Paris seduced Helen and took her with him back to Troy. A ten-year siege of Troy finally ended in victory for the Greeks, largely because of Odysseus's wily stratagem of a soldier-filled war machine in the shape of a horse. After their victory, most of the Greek warriors returned to their various homes.

As the story of the *Odyssey* begins, an additional ten years have passed but Odysseus still has not returned to his home on the island of Ithaca. On his journey home, he has been harassed repeatedly by Poseidon, the god of the sea who angrily seeks revenge for old affronts to his honor. Truth to tell, Odysseus himself has seemed at times in no particular hurry to return home. He spent an extended holiday in the embraces of a mysterious enchantress named Circe. Although, in fairness, he did lack transportation, he passed some seven more years ensconced on a secluded island with the beautiful nymph Calypso.

When we first meet Odysseus in the epic, however, he is sitting alone on the seashore of Calypso's island, Ogygia, weeping as he gazes over the limitless waves in the direction of home. He feels lost and immobilized. Delicate negotiations on his behalf are going on at the divine level between Athena and Zeus. The outcome of these negotiations will set him back in motion toward who he is and where he longs to be.

By now Odysseus has been away from Ithaca for twenty years. During the last ten, no one at home has known whether he is dead or alive. The situation in the palace is intolerable. Odysseus's only child Telemachus, left as an infant when his father went to war, has been raised alone by a mother who sees her authority over her son slipping away. Telemachus's status is ambiguous, or rather, he has no status at all. He is neither adult nor child, neither the new male head of the household nor the son of a merely absent father. He is mostly ignored by his mother's suitors, when they are not hurling abuse at him. Telemachus soon will have to leave home on a long and dangerous journey to find news of his father and to discover himself.

Penelope stays at home—anxious mother, neither wife nor widow, object of repellent proposals—and faces the hardest straits of all. Always she grieves for her husband, though she gave up long ago any real hope for his return. At the same time, she has sole responsibility for keeping the household financially intact, especially since the one family member who could have helped her, her father-in-law Laertes, has long since removed himself to an outlying shepherd's hut. Every night the licentious suitors help themselves to a feast in the great hall of the palace, taunting Penelope to choose which one of them she will marry.

Now she watches her son Telemachus become ever more distant, more listless and depressed. Even in the best of circumstances she alone could not have ushered Telemachus into adulthood. Now she is helpless, and because Telemachus is insecure, he is prickly toward her as well as himself.

All of this turmoil brings Athena down from Mount Olympus. In the anthropomorphism of the earliest Greek epics, gods play favorites. Like mortals, the gods help their friends and harm their enemies. Athena has long been the special protector of Odysseus and his family, so it is not remarkable that she will help out now.

What may not be anticipated by modern readers is that Athena almost always comes unbidden to each of the three major figures in the epic. She does not need to be invoked or prayed to in any formal or informal way. She is always standing by, on the lookout for the well-being of those she cares most about. And when she comes, she never asks "What can I do to help?" She just helps.

The story moves along with the limited but timely appearances of Athena in her array of disguises. With "Mentor" on the ship bench beside him, Telemachus embarks on his long and successful journey toward adulthood. Odysseus finally arrives home in Ithaca with help from the goddess. Penelope recovers her native strength after a nighttime visit from Athena, disguised as Penelope's sister Iphthime, whom she has hardly seen since she married Odysseus and moved to Ithaca many years before.

After all the reunions on Ithaca, Odysseus joins with Telemachus and with his father Laertes, now out of retirement, to kill the rude suitors who have been devouring his goods and threatening his wife. The suitors' families arm themselves for a showdown with Odysseus, and it seems that the bloodletting will never stop. At that moment, Athena makes her last appearance, standing between the two camps and proclaiming an end to the fighting. The parties agree. This goddess, a lover of peace, although ready to fight when required, assumes the role of wise peacemaker in her community. Homer tells us that until the end of the story, Athena retained the face and form of Mentor.

2

THE
ATTENTIVE ELDER

*Athena came to his prayer from close at hand, for all the world with
Mentor's build and voice, and she urged him on with winged words:
"Telemachus, you'll lack neither courage nor sense from this day
on, not if your father's spirit courses through your veins."*

Odyssey 2.300–304

*The prince replied, wise in his own way too, "How can I greet him,
Mentor, even approach the king? I'm hardly adept at subtle conversation. Someone my age might feel shy, what's more, interro-
gating an older man."*

*"Telemachus," the bright-eyed goddess Athena reassured him,
"some of the words you'll find within yourself, the rest some power
will inspire you to say. You least of all—I know—were born and
reared without the gods' good will."*

Odyssey 3.23–32

When Athena appears in Ithaca disguised as
Mentor, the first to notice a visitor at the
threshold is young Telemachus. He has been
sitting idly among the suitors, defeated by grief and day-

dreaming about how his father Odysseus would set everything in order again if only he could magically drop down from the clouds.

When Telemachus sees Mentes, he hurries to greet him and promises a royal welcome into the household. "Have supper first," he says, "then tell us what you need" (1.145–47). Telemachus finds Mentes a chair of honor, draws up a low stool beside him, and summons fine food and drink. After the suitors swagger in and tune up their revelry, Telemachus leans close and begins to angle for news of his father. Mentes answers in a kind of doublespeak, encouraging the young man to think his father is still alive even while counseling him to undertake a long journey in pursuit of news of him. Talk turns to the despicable suitors. Mentes advises Telemachus to summon an assembly and announce that the suitors must return to their homes. When the stranger rises to leave, Telemachus offers him a fine gift, another convention of ancient hospitality. It will be, he says, "the kind of gift / a host will give a stranger, friend to friend" (3.358–60).

The arrival of a kindly stranger heartens Telemachus first because it enables him to function as an adult. He serves as host in place of his parent, literally *in loco parentis*. The most notable quality of this interaction is the mutual respect between host and guest. It is a new and bracing experience for Telemachus to be treated not as a child or as someone's son but as an adult whose ideas are important.

The next morning he summons the people to attend a full assembly, the first to be called on the island since Odysseus sailed away. Telemachus finds his voice, assumes his authority, and proclaims that the suitors must leave the palace and go home. Everyone is amazed at his new sense of command. The hecklers soon begin their taunts and challenges nevertheless, and eventually the assembly breaks up. The suitors amble back to the palace.

Having taken his first stand, Telemachus is scared to death. He goes alone to seek solace on the seashore, where Athena is standing by and approaches him in the form of the old family friend. Mentor assures Telemachus that his father's courage and intelligence are his qualities too, manifest from this day on. For now, she says, they have work to do: Telemachus is to go prepare rations for their journey while she recruits a crew for the ship.

Mentor accompanies Telemachus on the voyage from Ithaca to Pylos, home of the aged King Nestor who had been at Troy and might have news of Odysseus. Telemachus is nervous about his first foray into public diplomacy. What shall he say to the king? And is it not presumptuous for the young to query their elders at all? Mentor assures Telemachus that his intelligence will give him the words he needs and that some further power (*daimon*) will help him as well.

Three details in this interaction between Telemachus and Athena as the old family friend characterize their relationship. The first is that Mentor is standing nearby, already on the lookout for the younger man's needs. The second is that she offers encouragement, but quickly turns to practical plans for dealing with the dilemma. Finally, when Telemachus asks what he should say when he faces King Nestor, Mentor does not hand him a script. She responds simply that the young man's own intelligence and insight will provide what he needs to make it through the ordeal. In short, Telemachus can do it himself.

As long as I thought that mentors had to be men, I felt bereft and lonely, often doubting if I could "do it myself." Unknowingly I had incorporated the mores of the culture around me. When the story of Athena in the *Odyssey* finally made its full impression, however, I began to recognize the mentors already at my side.

Mary Louise:
Mentor of Mind and Heart

I came to see that Mary Louise Brewer had been watching out for me from my earliest memory. While I was still very young, my mother would take me to the apartment downtown where Mary Louise lived with her husband and small daughter. Those visits were magical for me. Mary Louise would scour the alley behind the local department store, gathering castoff store decorations for us to reassemble into our own colorful creations. We made cookies. We played tea party. We told stories. Many years later, when my daughter went with me to visit Mary Louise for tea, I saw the same enchantment in Carrie's eyes that filled mine as a child.

Almost from the beginning, I associated Mary Louise with the written word. I still have a little book she made for me when I was isolated with German measles at about seven or eight years old. It is a spiral notebook with pictures from magazines pasted in it, each captioned with handwritten comments about people and events in my life.

When I was an adolescent Mary Louise and her family moved to a house directly across the alley from us. During those years while I was still at home, she continued my education. Once when a great actress—I think it was Helen Hayes—came to read scenes from Shakespeare at the nearby college, Mary Louise called ahead to find out what passages would be read. Then she invited me over the afternoon before the performance with one or two others to read the scenes aloud. That experience imprinted on me permanently one of the joys of the life of the mind.

During my college years some of the values I learned in my hometown separated me from some of its entrenched customs. In these times, Mary Louise always provided a haven. She cheered when I quarreled with my sorority over its racial and class exclusions, and she understood when I participated in student demonstrations at the local movie theaters and restaurants against racial segregation—activities that did not come easily for me and caused painful divisions among my friends and within my family. (My father said he would meet me on the other side of the barricade. My mother, happily, had no such problems supporting me in this matter.) I always expected that, in the end, both my parents would support me after I made hard choices, such as deciding to pursue a Ph.D. I always suspected that Mary Louise would agree with me.

During college I began to travel and thus to share another great love of Mary Louise's life. On a glorious day in June, after my first year in college, my mother and I set out on our first travel abroad. As we entered our cabin on the ocean liner that would take us to Greece, a bon voyage letter from Mary Louise was propped on the dresser. I was impressed that anyone knew how to send a letter to a ship.

Three years later, Mary Louise and her daughter joined my mother and me for another journey to Greece. As we walked the streets of Athens, three of the four of us spoke of the Latin we learned from Harry Leon at the University of Texas over a period of more than thirty years. Dr. Leon directed Mary Louise's doctoral dissertation. He visited my mother at her dormitory infirmary when she was very ill. He nominated me for the fellowship that changed my life. He also had a puckish and unexpected sense of humor. On Dr. Leon's death, Mary Louise wrote of him: "I never knew a professor, or certainly never had one, the paradox of whose physical and mental qualities was so harmonious, whose unattractive physique was completely overshadowed and forgotten by a rapier-like mind and a knowledge and enthusiasm that projected ancient civilization in a marvelous way."

In my Methodist tradition we did not have godparents. So, on a radiant summer day on the island of Aegina, I lowered my head near the columns of the Temple of Aphaia, bathed in the peculiar lucidity of the Greek light. Mary Louise placed handpicked laurel leaves upon my brow, and there we proclaimed ourselves honorary godmother and goddaughter.

Immediately after that journey I started graduate school. Those years were hard, not so much because of the study but because I never had a female professor and could not quite figure out how to be one. Mary Louise gave me courage. She was at that time the only woman I knew who had earned a Ph.D. and married and had children too. At the age of thirty-five she had been, in her own words, "old maid, sweetheart, wife, and mother, all in one year."

Before that, Mary Louise had finished college in Oklahoma, taught school, received an M.A. in classics at the University of Illinois—arriving there with what one of her professors called "a resume as long as the Tiber"—then earned a Ph.D. at the University of Texas with a dissertation on the poetry of Spenser and Petrarch. Before she met her husband, she taught at Texas Tech and also traveled the world on tramp steamers. When my husband Ashley and I honeymooned on the Malaysian island of Penang in the Strait of Malacca, Mary Louise was the only person I knew who had been there.

Mary stopped teaching the year she married and did not resume until after the death of her husband, so I did not benefit even here from watching a woman I admired living the life that I sought both at work and at home. Nevertheless, I learned how to teach from Mary Louise. She taught me to make connections and to divide a class for discussion. She urged the "twenty minute rule," that is, to vary the pace of an hour-long class by dividing the time into three parts. To this day, twenty minutes is as long as I like to speak continuously in any forum. From Mary Louise I also learned to wear pretty colors in the classroom, not for ourselves but for the benefit of our students, who have to look at us.

In a letter to me after a long talk about life in the academy, Mary Louise wrote: "I've thought over many of the problems and puzzles of academic life you posed and believe we came to some logical conclusions. To concentrate on where your gifts and satisfactions lie was one of them."

Throughout her life Mary Louise has never been afraid to do new, hard things. In my files I have her published paper, "Franz Kafka: His Place in World Literature." She wrote that paper in her late sixties for an academic conference, a completely new subject for her. Kafka is hard for anyone at any age, but she took him on, journeyed with him into strange and distant worlds, then made him her own by connecting him with what she already knew. The opening sentence of this paper also describes its author: "Like Proteus, Kafka changes shape with each literary comparison."

Mary Louise is now in her nineties. She stretches her mind every day by reading, writing, thinking, and conversation. She is a woman of faith, free of dogma and self-righteousness. She creates a caring and engaged community around her wherever she is. Her hopes for the world are undimmed.

In a letter to me on my birthday, an occasion she never fails to mark, Mary Louise wrote: "As you look back over your birthdays, I wonder what vision of life you now have—in defining the *summum bonum* of your days."

When Mary Louise pruned her library for a move, she sent me some of her Greek and Latin texts. I have studied and taught the same authors, but more endearing to me are the inside pages inscribed with her name and whereabouts: Vergil's *Aeneid,* Ardmore High School, 1924; Lucretius's *De Rerum Natura,* Oklahoma College for Women, 1928 (with a note added that she was serving as student body president that year), along with an additional address at the University of Illinois, Champaign-Urbana, 1929; and finally, a Latin-

English dictionary inscribed with her name and the address of the University Faculty Women's Club, Austin, Texas.

It was almost my own journey, years later and with the order reversed: I was graduated from college at the University of Texas in Austin, and my first teaching position was in Champaign-Urbana at the University of Illinois.

So there was Mary Louise, right across the alley in Lubbock, Texas, paying attention to me my whole life through. All the while, she was nurturing with mind and heart the subjects I loved and the choices I made.

Rachel
Writer as Mentor

Then there was Rachel. Rachel was different from anyone I have ever known.

At the other end of Houston County from our farm in middle Tennessee, under three oak trees standing sentinel over a ruined peach and apple orchard, stands a small tombstone with the epitaph: "Dear friend, whoever you are, take this kiss." The words are from Walt Whitman. A wild blackberry bush grows on the grave. Rachel chose the inscription herself. She would like the wild blackberry bush.

I first heard of Rachel Maddux from Quaker friends who spoke of a writer in rural Tennessee who sometimes attended their Friends Meeting in Nashville. Several years later I read her fourth novel, *A Walk in the Spring Rain*, and saw in the credits her expression of gratitude to the agricultural agent of our county for his help in identifying the fauna and flora in the book. As soon as I realized Rachel was the writer and she lived nearby, I drove over to the orchard one Sunday afternoon to meet her.

She and her husband, King Baker, were away, but a young

man tending the orchard and house in their absence invited me in to leave a note. The first thing I noticed was a framed photograph of Ingrid Bergman, taken while she and Anthony Quinn were filming *A Walk in the Spring Rain*. (Later when I helped prepare Rachel's papers for the Special Collections Library at Boston University, I found a file of affectionate letters sent by Bergman to Rachel from all over the world.) In the photograph, her face is radiant and her arms are around Rachel's goats.

But I knew about the goats already. In *A Walk in the Spring Rain*, Will Workman speaks about them with Libby Meredith:

"I suppose you got a word for that," he said.

"For what?"

"For the way you love them goats," he said. "For the soft hand."

"Oh, tenderness, I suppose," I said, feeling my eyes suddenly burn with the excess I know myself to have of it, so that I would pour it out on strangers if it were not that I know they would call the police or turn from me in fear. It has grown so much greater in me in the last years, this awful flood. . . . Oh, isn't it sad that in our world it is so hard to give it? God knows people need it.

The next week I showed up unannounced at her door. Rachel welcomed me as calmly as if she had been waiting and offered a glass of cool spring water. With a simple gesture she motioned for me to sit down with her at the dining table. Immediately we became immersed in a conversation about creativity in children. Rachel was certain that children are born creative and are educated out of it. I have since seen research confirming her certainty, that most children are creative at the age of two and most are not by the age of fifteen.

My friendship with Rachel began the day we met and lasted until her death seven years later. Once or twice a month I would drive to the orchard on a Sunday afternoon for conversation, often jotting her observations in a small notebook in my lap. Sometimes I took special friends to meet Rachel. Frequently I met friends of hers who also had come to visit.

Our first conversation returned to mind several years later when I was pontificating to Rachel about how one has to kill off one's poetic father in order to become a poet oneself. This was in the first and fleeting flush of my "Harold Bloom stage" concerning the anxiety of influence.

"No," said Rachel after a gravid pause. "You must become your own child." The childlikeness she honored as essential to creativity had to do, I think, with the fact that children have not yet substituted abstractions and ideology—both of which foster conformity—for attachment to individuals and elemental fairness.

But that is not how Rachel said it. Instead, she said it this way: "Now, I have got a theory too. It may be lots of other people's too, but I think it's mine. I believe that inspiration is the recapturing of one's childhood. In childhood, there is a continual teeter-totter of the real and the imaginary, the subconscious and the conscious mind."

Creativity, profoundly bound with love for people and a sense of justice, defined Rachel's life and work.

Rachel and King moved to middle Tennessee from Los Angeles in 1960. In a 1977 interview she explained: "King had a dream for an apple orchard in Tennessee. We said we wanted to have a try at fighting nature instead of our fellow man, a battle for which we are both ill suited." For her the two battles would be interrelated, which is the story of her only nonfiction work, *The Orchard Children*, later made into a TV docudrama by CBS. But King told me once that the orchard saved his life, and Rachel said she could live anywhere, so this is where they were.

Rachel was born in Wichita, Kansas, in 1913. After receiving a B.A. from the University of Kansas at Lawrence in 1934 and attending medical school for a time, she moved to

Kansas City where she lived, except for a brief stay in Los Angeles, until her marriage to King Baker shortly before World War II. After the war, Rachel and King eventually settled in Los Angeles. Rachel was proud of saying that in twenty-five moves during the decade and a half she was writing her major work, *The Green Kingdom*, published in 1957, she never lost a page of the manuscript.

In his memoir about Kansas City journalism in the thirties, Martin Quigley recalls the gatherings of young writers at Rachel's apartment at 16 West 43rd, which he called "the only Bohemia in town." Rachel urged the group gathered around her to produce a literary journal. The journal never appeared, but it was in that apartment that Rachel wrote *Turnip's Blood*, the work that established her as a writer. "She was a beautiful Junoesque young woman with long reddish-blond hair," says Quigley. "A reclusive mystic with a slow sweet smile and instant sensitivity, she was wise and gifted and made us feel wise and gifted."

Rachel made everyone around her feel wise and gifted. She did not so much bring out the best in people as bring out something they did not know was there. Rachel did occasionally complain about would-be writers calling on her for help—not with writing but with publishing. In this regard she said she felt surrounded by chickens pecking for corn, quoting, I think, Edna St. Vincent Millay.

What I saw, however, was the limitless hospitality framed in her epitaph. I know at least a dozen people who, like me, thought of themselves as her dearest friend. She would ask guests to sign a red tablecloth after a meal, then later would embroider their names in white as a permanent record of their visit. She loved to offer special guests a hot towel steamed in scented water and presented in a domed silver butter dish. She never turned away a stranger or a stray animal.

Rachel wrote her autobiography, *Communication: Being the*

Mental Autobiography of a Sturdy Quest, in 1941 at the improbable age of twenty-eight. That it was published posthumously, fifty years later, would not have surprised its author. She said to aspiring writers, "You do what you have to do, that's all, for as long as you are able, and if you do it well, it may live after you. But if it doesn't, why, you do it anyway." Another time she said to me simply, "If it is not published in your lifetime, then your daughter will publish it, or your granddaughter."

In *Communication* Rachel indulges in none of the nostalgia or sentimentality about childhood that often masks unacknowledged anger. Instead, she recreates with brutal honesty her determination from her earliest years not to give in to the isolation surrounding what we would now recognize as a peculiarly gifted child. She writes in the preface: "This is the story of a long and discouraging search for communication with a human being, for the recognition of someone else who was *attentive* to the same things *in the same way,* for another mind that could not fool itself."

At the age of three or four Rachel took her first determined step toward communication. If she could read, she reasoned, she would have all the knowledge that other people around her seemed to have. "I had affection and love but no communication and I soon discovered why. The great thing I lacked that other people had was a knowledge of reading. How simple. I would learn to read, then I would also know everything."

This is how she taught herself to read: First she insisted that her parents read to her only one children's book, *Peter and Polly,* until she knew it by heart. Then she went through a newspaper story until she found a word she recognized, returning to her memorized children's book until she found a correspondence in "the eighth word from the left, line 2, page 24, of *Peter and Polly.*" She repeated this process over and over until she knew by sight enough words in the book to be able to fill in the gaps by asking the meaning of the remaining ones.

When her formal education began at the age of five, she was astonished to learn about spelling. "I was amazed," she remembers, "for I thought that books had always existed and that all people had to teach themselves to read as I had."

In her teens Rachel would read as many as twenty books a week. When I knew her she still was reading voluminously. Somehow she was able to find nearly everything she wanted through the regional library system, and there was always a stack of new books on the table by her fireplace at the orchard. The stories of Isaac Bashevis Singer were a special favorite. Of Alice Walker's *The Color Purple*, she commented: "How rare in a novel to watch characters grow." In *Communication* she says that she always tried to read books in one sitting "with a feeling of responsibility to the author."

Reading did not bring communication for Rachel. She did not yet have a listener, but in high school she did meet Hugh, a fellow student who read the *New York Times* and the *New Yorker*, who knew what plays were on Broadway that very night, and who taught her that literature was not dead.

> Hugh knew literature, and he taught me, without ever saying so, that it can change and be new all the time, that it is very much a part of daily life, and that the plot is *not* the thing. He knew about Sherwood Anderson and *Winesburg, Ohio*. I cannot begin to tell you what that book meant to me, those stories about people *just like the ones I knew*, those very simple stories, where the words coming out of people's mouths sounded just like the words coming out of people's mouths— not going through the author's head first.

Hugh, however, could talk only about literature, not about himself. "Most people do not have communication," she writes, "and they express this by saying they are not understood, putting all the responsibility on the listener, but the great responsibility is on the speaker, for when you get a listener you must be ready."

Rachel's quest for communication continued until she met the careful listener with a mind that could not fool itself, a literary agent in Hollywood to whom *Communication* is addressed. "By writing this to the only person in the world who could understand ALL of it *the way it is said,* I think I have learned how to write so that later things can be understood by any human being who has breathed the air in and breathed it out and learned to read and asked himself one question."

By the time Rachel wrote *Communication*, she was already an accomplished author. At the age of eleven she showed her first story to a family friend, who, she recalls, had the wisdom to send her away while he was reading it. Her novella *Turnip's Blood*, first published in *Story* magazine in 1936 and later anthologized in *The Flying Yorkshireman* in 1938, brought her a lifetime friendship with Savington Crampton, who was also the first to name and affirm her manner of writing.

Savington Crampton was en route from New York to Hollywood, where he produced the Benny Goodman show and other radio shows such as *The Camel Caravan,* when he stopped by Kansas City in 1937 to meet Rachel after reading *Turnip's Blood.* That was the beginning of a remarkable friendship that lasted until Rachel's death. A brilliant savant who still reads Latin for pleasure and exercises the same acute critical judgment that brought him to Rachel's door in Kansas City, Crampton always supported Rachel and her work. For example, she told him about a new part-time job with a real-estate company in Los Angeles after the war: "Here I am with another crummy job, Savvy," to which he replied, "You cannot afford a good job. It would cost too much."

Rachel tells in *Communication* about how she came to write *Turnip's Blood.* She was not writing and was not studying writing when she began to hear words spoken out loud. Eventually to get rid of them she wrote them down, only to be replaced by more words. When the words ended, the story ended. No word, she says, was ever chosen or changed. "When I read it over it amused me very much. I typed it off and sent it to my sister and told her how it had happened. She said I did not have to explain it, to go sit in the sun or eat a steak and leave it to her." She continued,

> It was published, and I had no idea that the process would re-peat itself, nor could I start it at will. Because it was published I met George [another producer, to whom *Communication* was addressed] and Savvy. . . . They were not interested in me be-cause I was strange or because I was strong or because of the reasons that other people were. They liked me because I was honest and because I was straightforward and because I could sit still. And they thought I was a writer. I would never have been able to say I was a writer when people asked me what I did. I said I worked in a paint store.

Then Rachel describes how a group of Savvy's friends gath-ered around her one afternoon in Hollywood and began to question her about *Turnip's Blood*.

> They asked me why I had written a certain line and what a cer-tain phrase meant and I was panic stricken, absolutely panic stricken, for I had never studied writing and I did not have the vocabulary for lying about it. I had my back against the wall and I finally said, I don't know what it means. I heard it spo-ken out loud by a voice and I copied it down. And I blushed scarlet because I was sure that they would all know immedi-ately that it was an hallucination and that it was only a symp-tom of the attacks—the awful, stupid way that I had heard people explain Van Gogh's painting entirely by his epilepsy.

After the people left, Savvy calmly persuaded her that she did not need to be embarrassed about the way she wrote. "It's just the inspirational method, that's all," he said. "The Bible was written that way and Blake wrote that way. Lots of people write by inspiration and some write by composition and some mix the two methods."

It was not long before she was writing again.

Savvy was not Rachel's Pygmalion, because she created herself. He did, however, confirm her vocation as a writer, he became one of the models for Justin Magnus in *The Green Kingdom*, and he stood by her as a friend and intellectual companion for forty-six years. "We were always a little ahead of each other," he recalls. "Nothing ever needed any footnotes." In a journal entry of 1946 Rachel noted: "I never feel really out of touch with Savvy. God love him. There is no one quite like him. There is no one who makes me feel quite so valuable— such an asset to the world."

That Rachel wrote by the inspirational method, as Savvy called it, may be partly explained by her extraordinary memory and her ear for music. In *Communication* she writes about a job she had during high school that required her to handle five telephones in addition to handling another task not related to the telephones. "I never got them mixed up," she writes. "Without trying to, I had memorized some 500 telephone numbers just by hearing them once."

She told me that she could hear the four symphonic movements of *The Green Kingdom* in her head as she wrote the novel. She loved to play piano duets with visitors and once induced me to play a Haydn duet with her, to my enormous surprise. Choral music formed a theme of her last work, an unfinished play entitled *Until the Clock Strikes*, and several times she asked me to find choral sheet music for her at the music library of my university. The most compelling evidence of the place of music in her creative imagination is in *Communication:*

> Later in another school I had a fine day. It grew out of a Greek sculpture class. I set the frieze on the Parthenon to music. I derived a constant measure for the vertical differences between head heights of the figures in the frieze and this constant I

represented by one note. The same applied to the hands.
There was a line of notes for the height of the heads and one
for the hands. The value of the note was determined by the
horizontal distance between the figures, as measured against
that between the two closest. And put together, the heads line
and the hands line, you know what it played? It played a gentle, lovely melody exactly like a hymn.

Another source for Rachel's writing was her acute sensitivity to nature. Much of this came early with her discovery of
the French naturalist Fabre and his minute observations of the
whirling life contained in a tiny square of grass.

> For the communication with things other than people I have
> to thank Mr. Fabre and I wish he were not so long dead. I wish
> I could thank him personally. For a landscape no longer looks
> like a picture postcard to me, static and finished and still. I no
> longer see a tree and over it the sky and under it the grass.
> Many many [sic] things are *going on* in that landscape and now
> I know it all the time. I look. Even looking from a distance I
> know it. For in the tree is a bird and on the bird is a louse and
> on the louse are bacteria. And from the branches of the tree
> hang beautiful complex spider webs and in the tree is a spider
> with her foot upon a sensitive telegraph wire attached to the
> web at the place of maximum communication.

Rachel's attachment to nature was not only philosophical
but also practical and practiced. One glorious summer afternoon she rode through back country Tennessee roads with
my daughter Carrie and me to pick wildflowers. As we picked,
she named them all: bergamot, blackeyed Susans, butterfly's
breath, elderberry vine, purple phlox, Queen Anne's lace,
trumpet vine. And it was she who taught me the secret of
adding redbud blossoms to salads at Easter time.

Rachel's writing rose also out of her courage and her un-
reasonable love for the world. She summarized her religion in
three words: "Everyone is me." Her definition of human rights

was equally terse: "It's a pretty hard passage down the birth canal, and anyone who makes it has a right to be here."

Her conscience authenticated her writing. She learned early the power of the written word. In *Communication* she says that as a child she read in the newspaper about an execution scheduled to take place that day at midnight:

> I lay in bed thinking it is ten o'clock. He has two hours. Now it is 10:15. Now it is 10:30. By midnight I had a headache so violent I do not think I was quite sane. And one minute after midnight I tried and tried to realize as my own knowledge that a man was not in the world where, one minute before, he had been. I was ashamed of myself, that I had read about it and then just lain in bed, that I had LET that thing happen. I should have run to Topeka and clawed and scratched at the governor until he stopped it.
>
> This feeling of responsibility held over me and later I actually did write a letter to the governor about a man who was to receive a long term for his fourth or fifth offence of stealing chickens to feed his motherless children. I got a letter from the governor and the man got pardoned, though I never knew him, and I was very much impressed by this, by what could be accomplished with the written word by a child when nobody will listen to the *spoken* word.
>
> This writing, I thought, is a serious thing, not to be fooled around with. Perhaps that is where my respect for the written word comes from.

Rachel wrote also out of her adamant refusal ever to hide from her loneliness or to divide private life from public. "To write," she said to me once, "you have to be willing to lie naked on the dining room table in the middle of the interstate." On another occasion she said, "To be able to write exquisitely with a spider eating each word as it is formed, that is for me. To live in the middle of absolute inconsequence, believing that what I do matters absolutely, that is the biggest joke of all."

Rachel was very much a public citizen, from her precinct organizing for Adlai Stevenson in Los Angeles to her advocacy for civil rights in rural middle Tennessee. She and King were among the few white supporters of integration in their county during their early days in Tennessee. There were consequences. Rachel had organized a Girl Scout troop for young African American girls two or three years after they arrived. After a few meetings, someone drove up and down the rows of fruit trees King had so carefully planted, breaking down all of them.

Rachel's racial sensitivities had been sealed long before in her friendship with a young black woman in Occoquan, Virginia, fictionalized in her novel *Abel's Daughter*. Among Rachel's papers is a file of correspondence from that friend, called Serena in the novel, who later named a daughter after Rachel.

King's and Rachel's neighbors near the orchard eventually came to accept them, and some became devoted to Rachel. Lydia Belle, a beloved friend who lived on a hardscrabble farm nearby and once took tatting lessons with Rachel, lovingly made a quilted piecework vest for her. One of the last outings Rachel and I made was to Lydia Belle's for a fitting of the vest.

Rachel may have written by the inspirational method, but she was quite clearheaded about the creative process. "Write with your creative self," she urged me. "Then go over it again with your corrective self." Once she admonished me perceptively, "Creativity is not subject to control. And I imagine it's hard for you to give up control." She warned never to make excuses for not writing and in particular to avoid the "cabin in the woods" syndrome, as in "I could write if only I had a cabin in the woods." "The demands of one's own work," she remarked on one occasion, "unlike those sometimes imposed by other people, never seem outrageous. 'Yassuh,' we say obsequiously, 'Yassuh.' Shuffle, shuffle."

In the early years when my scholarly writing was excruciatingly slow, she encouraged me by saying that perhaps this writing was practice for something I might want to do later. Perhaps her most encouraging words were these: "The difficult thing isn't writing. That's easy. The difficult thing is waiting to write." It took Rachel over a decade to be able to write about the events described in *The Orchard Children*. Before that, she said, she was not able to leave out enough.

In the years I knew Rachel she wrote between 2:00 and 4:00 A.M. She wrote everything first in a fine longhand, usually in unlined bound notebooks, then typed out the final copy on her ancient Royal upright typewriter. Both the manuscripts and typescripts show evidence of correction and revision, but not much. She was an expert typist, which was a good thing given the fate of *The Green Kingdom*.

This major novel was rejected thirteen times before Simon and Schuster expressed an interest in it. They said, however, that it was twice as long as it should be. Rachel simply retyped the manuscript, narrowing the margins but not leaving out a word, and resubmitted it. It was accepted. The published version of *The Green Kingdom* is 561 pages long.

Creativity is measured by one's response to failure, not to success. Failure is a sign of one's willingness to take risks. In sorting Rachel's papers I found a large piece of poster board, carefully marked into a grid. In the left-hand column were the names of five or six short stories she had sent out for publication. There was another column for the date mailed, another for the cost of the postage, still another for the date receipt of the manuscript was acknowledged. The final column was headed "Accepted or rejected." All the stories had been rejected.

Years later I was with Rachel when she opened a letter from her agent who had been trying unsuccessfully to place one of her stories. The letter consisted of four words: "I don't give up."

"Ah," smiled Rachel, "those wonderful four-word letters."

A careless observer could confuse Rachel's tenderness with pessimism. She said once to me, "Life after all is fair; ultimately it breaks everybody's heart." And in *A Walk in the Spring Rain* she writes of her discovery of the truth that "agony takes precedence." Rachel's writing and life, however, were braced with remarkable resilience and laced with humor. After King's death the orchard froze for two successive years and she was in desperate financial straits. She never gave up. "I'm going to write my way out of this," she said through clenched teeth.

Her humor was in-wrought with her wry insight about the human condition. "When I am dictator . . ." she liked to intone with a grin whenever she heard of some egregious injustice. She was quick-witted too. Once when a potential biographer asked her if she believed in heaven, she demurred. He pressed her, "Well, if you did, whom would you want to see there?" Instantly she replied, "You mean after former lovers?"

Rachel taught me by her tenderness and love, her relentless care with the written and spoken word, and her lifetime play of showdown hands. Pain was her teacher, and she was patient enough to wait for the truth and the words. But she also believed we are meant to be happy. I cannot say whether at the end she *was* happy. She was, however, "grappling rather than buffeted"—the condition she identifies in the preface to *The Green Kingdom* as constituting the climate of potentiality.

In *Communication* Rachel wrote of her pleasure as a very young woman at being recognized as a writer by her new circle of friends in California, but she knew that the danger was great that she would accumulate too soon what she calls a series of possessions and the competitive spirit. "And I knew," she says, "I must take my new confidence and my new happiness and my new stillness and my new stories and go home *where I knew who I was* while I waited for the maturation."

During her last illness Rachel asked me to find a recording

of the musical *Carnival*, in which the character Lilly sings of coming from a town called Mira "where everybody knew my name." I played a cassette of the recording for Rachel in the intensive care room of the tiny country hospital where she drifted in and out of consciousness, every breath a contest with the cancer that was consuming her. Remembering that she had told me that hearing was the last sense to leave a dying person, I said, "Rachel, you have written beautiful books, you have touched a thousand lives, and a lot of people know your name."

She smiled, her eyes closed, and she said, "Yes, it's nice, isn't it?"

Rachel Maddux died two days later.

In the years I knew Rachel, Savvy called her faithfully at the orchard every Sunday afternoon at 3:00 P.M. The two did not, however, see eye to eye on every issue. Rachel recounted to me one of the Sunday conversations shortly after seeing television documentaries about Golda Meir and then-Connecticut governor Ella Grasso. Rachel asked Savvy what he thought about them. Not much, he said. Then, a little impatient, she pressed the issue.

"Well, has there ever been a woman in public life you admired?" she asked.

"Yes, one," he answered.

"Who?" she asked.

"Athena," he said.

Mary Louise and Rachel ushered me into maturity. One was there from the beginning, helping form the paths I would take. The other appeared at the moment I needed her. They were my friends too, but they were and are more than that. They were the attentive elders standing by, looking out for my well-being with only my interest and not their own at heart. One of them confirmed my vocation. The other gave me courage for my craft.

These mentors were not perfect, of course. The gifts they offered me, however, were perfect for me at the time I needed them. Athena herself was not perfect. The Greeks devised gods very much like ourselves, after all, and Athena could be both vain and jealous. For example, after Pan got tired of his pipes and threw them down, Athena picked them up and decided to take up music. She enjoyed practicing until the day she saw her reflection while playing the pipes and was appalled at how the effort distorted her beautiful face. So she quit.

Then there is the problem of the spider. The Roman poet Ovid tells the story of Arachne, a young Lydian woman who boasted that her weaving rivaled that of Athena. In the disguise of an old woman Athena paid a visit to Arachne and cautioned her against the pride of such presumption. A contest ensued, and when Athena realized that the young woman's weaving was in fact as good as her own, she flew into such a rage that Arachne hanged herself. Thereafter she was turned by Athena into a spider—still good at weaving.

In the *Odyssey* Telemachus rarely realizes that it is Athena at his side until after she has departed. Odysseus, on the other hand, usually sees through her disguises so quickly they both laugh about it.

I wonder if this recognition is something we get better at with practice. Whereas years ago I thought I had no mentors at all, now I recognize them all around. My guess is that this has something to do with time on the road and with our own security. The more we have been nurtured and cared for, the more open we are to receiving.

Among my attentive elders, those sufficiently older to be always ahead of me, I can think of at least four in the town where I live. Three are writers. The other is a professor nearing ninety who is just beginning to retire. None of the four ever helped me "get ahead" in anything. I don't remember ever asking a favor of any of them, although I probably have. They, on the other hand, have each offered help to me in ways that I never expected. I sense that they are looking out for my well-being when I am not even aware of it. Maybe I think this because one of them sometimes calls me out of the blue for a "mental health checkup."

These four mentors share several qualities in common. They never condescend to me. I feel neither deferential to them nor somehow in their debt. I respect their judgment implicitly. I value their views and feel free to hold close to my own. They are all political, which is to say they are deeply committed to the well-being of the world. That is why they want me to succeed—for the sake of the world. All have suffered great slings, but none is defeated. To be in their company is a joy.

These mentors are my companions for the duration. It pleases me to add that three of the four of them are men. Sometimes good men walk around disguised as Athena.

3

FAMILY
MEMBERS

And again the bright-eyed goddess Pallas thought of one more way to help. She made a phantom now, its build like a woman's build, Iphthime's, yes, another daughter of generous Lord Icarius, Eumelus' bride, who made her home in Pherae. Athena sped her on to King Odysseus' house to spare Penelope, worn with pain and sobbing, further spells of grief and storms of tears. The phantom entered her bedroom, passing quickly in through the doorbolt slit and hovering at her head she rose and spoke now: "Sleeping, Penelope, your heart so wrung with sorrow? No need, I tell you, no, the gods who live at ease can't bear to let you weep and rack your spirit. Your son will still come home—it is decreed. He's never wronged the gods in any way."

Odyssey 4.893–908

thena appears only once in the *Odyssey* in the guise of a family member. When she does, she comes as a sibling. Penelope desperately needs comfort. She has just learned that Telemachus has left home on a long and treacherous journey without telling her he was going. She is terrified she will lose her son as she assumes she has lost her husband.

Having thought of "one more way to help," Athena assumes the form of Penelope's sister Iphthime. Penelope has hardly seen her beloved sister since she herself married and left the home of her father, Icarius. Iphthime glides into Penelope's chambers, awakens her from her troubled sleep, and assures her that Telemachus will return home safely.

The two talk for a while. It is clear how much Penelope misses her beloved Iphthime. "You live so far away," she laments. But she chides her sister, is almost angry with her, for telling her to put away her fears. How could she do that, she asks, with her husband lost years ago and now her child gone too. She says that Telemachus is in such great danger that she mourns him even more than her husband:

> And now my darling boy, he's off and gone in a hollow ship! Just a
> youngster, still untrained for war or stiff debate. Him, I mourn
> even more than I do my husband—quake in terror for all that he
> might suffer either on open sea or shores he goes to visit.

> Odyssey 4.919–24

Iphthime persists in her encouragement. This time she adds evidence for her confidence about the safety of Telemachus. He has someone at his side, she says, a companion whom anyone on earth would love to have nearby: Athena herself. Furthermore, it was Athena who sent Iphthime to Ithaca to stand by her in her anguish:

> "Courage!" the shadowy phantom reassured her. "Don't be over-
> whelmed by all your direst fears. He travels with such an escort,
> one that others would pray to stand beside them. She has power—
> Pallas Athena. She pities you in your tears. She wings me here to
> tell you all these things."

> Odyssey 4.928–33

With this Penelope begins to surmise that maybe more is going on here than she thought. Guessing that it may be a divinity at her side, she broaches the subject of Odysseus's fate. Athena has done what she came to do, however, and leaves Penelope's chambers the way she came in, as only a god could do, through the keyhole: "She glided off by the doorpost past the bolt—gone on a lifting breeze."

Mentors in the Family

Penelope's concern about the fate of her son is overwhelming, understandable, and appropriate. She has no distance or objectivity about her child, nor should she. In the classical model, parents are not mentors to their children. Perhaps this is as well, considering all their other responsibilities: physical safety, food and shelter, education, instruction and advice, modeling of family relationships, introductions to the larger world.

Parents are role models for their children, for ill or good. At their best they are the best of teachers. The father of one of my students, for example, asked his son all through college not, "What grades are you making?" but "Did you ask an interesting question today?"

Still, parents have a profound investment in the outcome of their children, as well they should. If they do not, who will? And if they do not hope that their children turn out pretty much like themselves, they have resisted a great temptation.

Mentors help others to identify and realize their hopes, but they are never personally invested in the outcome. They do not need the other to become like themselves. In the classical model of mentoring, an unrelated adult, or even a relative at a slightly greater remove, may fill that role more easily.

Nor, in the classical model, are spouses or partners mentors to one another. Such relationships have financial, moral, and emotional obligations, often girded by legal status and/or religious belief. We are profoundly influenced by those with whom we share such bonds. Penelope is a true partner in her marriage with Odysseus, autonomous as well as committed. As Nancy Felson observes, Penelope shapes her own life story and controls the final outcome of her reunion with her husband in ways that signal true reciprocity. Relationships with mentors, however, are of a different order. They are a free thing, like a gift.

Even with these exceptions, many relatives remain on the mentor-eligibility roster: brothers and sisters, cousins, aunts, uncles, grandparents, and ancestors older still, even those no longer living. In one case I know, a friend's mother-in-law was her primary mentor. This list includes also our children, who are the subject of another chapter. We are responsible for them but they are not responsible for us. That is why their gifts of insight can come to us freely.

From this roster I begin where Homer does, with siblings. This subject must be approached with caution, because there are no guarantees. Cain and Abel, the first sibling pair in the biblical story, do not inspire our confidence in this matter. The same is true in the Greek tradition. In Homer's *Iliad*, Hector is a great warrior, his brother Paris a great lover. There is tension between them, and the actions of the latter eventually cause the death of the former. Greek tragic drama is about families, because that is where the good stories are.

Some brothers and sisters are so differently constructed, so contrary, sometimes even so full of antipathy toward one another that one wonders how they could be in the same family. Marguerite Yourcenar observes: "Anyone who thinks blood is thicker than water has never been present when a will is read."

Some of the power of sibling relationships is increasingly confirmed by science as well as stories. For his pioneering

study *Born to Rebel* (1996), Frank J. Sulloway created a com-
puterized model out of his close scrutiny of six thousand lives
in western history since the sixteenth century. He shows how
birth order and the resulting family dynamics affect such matters as creativity, the need to conform, and openness to new
ideas. Sulloway's preoccupation with this issue grew out of his
fascination with explaining the creative genius of Charles
Darwin (a fifth-born of six). By at least one reviewer, Sulloway's conclusions about the primacy of sibling relationships
have been compared in importance with those of Darwin for
our understanding of how the world works.

Sibling relationships, however important in our lives, are
still almost always the least recognized. When individuals die,
for example, sympathy centers on their parents or spouses or
children. Few attend to the grief of their surviving siblings,
who likely have had the longest and sometimes even the closest relationship of all. I came to see this at a conscious level
when I read Laura Palmer's account of her interviews with survivors of soldiers who had died in Vietnam:

> When I began research for this book, I expected to encounter
> people who would be unable to talk about the person they
> loved who died in Vietnam. I thought these people would
> most likely be mothers, but I was wrong. They were the broth-
> ers and sisters. I think their trauma is the least expressed. I
> think siblings are the least understood victims of the Vietnam
> War.

Each fall I teach a small seminar of college freshmen who
have left their homes only days or weeks before. Over and
over I am struck with the depth of their loyalty to their older
siblings or to younger ones they have just left behind. One student told how her little sister, with whom she shared a room,
woke up night after night with the same recurring nightmare,
that a wolf was climbing into the window. She would then

wake up her older sister for comfort. Who would comfort the little sister now?

An unusually perceptive and creative young woman, now a successful cartoonist, told another story. She had troubled dreams too, when she was nine or ten years old in her small Georgia town. Her scary dreams were not about wolves but about racial prejudice and fears that Hitler might come back. On these occasions her older brother would come to comfort her. The comfort was of two kinds. He would ask what she calls "security questions." In response she was supposed to describe things she could do in a dangerous situation to help keep herself and others safe. They would talk these solutions over together. His comfort was also material. He gave his sister a nickel for her really good answers to his questions and a penny for each pretty good answer. These coins she stored in a ceramic jar by her bed, yet another token of security.

This wise brother was equipping his sister to handle her fears by herself. He knew that the day would come when neither their parents nor he would be there to do it for her.

My younger brother was a significant mentor for me. He showed by example how to be effective in politics, how to host a good party, and how to care for family and friends. He had the rare gift of perfect timing and seemed always to be in the right place at the right time. While I was studying in New York, I decided one summer to take a train from Grand Central Station to Hereford, Texas, near our farm. When the train stopped briefly in Amarillo, I looked up in surprise to see an attractive young man walking through the observation car. It was John, who had driven to Amarillo to share with me the last stretch of the journey home.

Those who commit their lives to the arts are often particularly indebted to siblings. One thinks of Van Gogh, whose brother Theodore was always nearby, always supportive. Rachel Maddux said to young writers: "One gets quite a lot of help, one way or another. All the way, all the time, I have had my sister, Erma." Fugitive poet Allen Tate was supported financially by his businessman brother, Ben.

Gentle readers, you will have to supply your own mentor stories about cousins, uncles, or aunts. I do not have any, as both of my parents were only children. Often I longed for a wise aunt, preferably one a little on the wacky side. It was Auntie Mame, after all, who took her young nephew on splendid adventures around the world and taught him how to make the perfect martini.

One event in particular demonstrated to me the importance of these relatives at one remove. When the Lambda Association at my university invited me to speak, I talked about how helpful brothers and sisters can be when a family is regrouping around knowledge that a member is lesbian or gay. Afterwards one of the young women asked me, "What about cousins?" She described her anxiety about how to tell her parents that she was lesbian. Full of fear, she approached one of her cousins instead. The cousin laughed and said, "Oh, that's all right. I'm lesbian too."

A mother-in-law might not come first to mind as a mentor, but for my friend Anne Roos this is the case. Anne says she learned three things from her mother-in-law. The first is to "broaden the matrix." When faced with a problem, enlarge the context in which it is framed. Second, learn to move quickly when a need or opportunity presents itself. Finally, know how to raise money for the purposes you care about. Over and over I have observed Anne living these precepts in her own life. For just one example, she is the person singularly responsible for Alan Le Quire's monumental statue of Athena in the Nashville Parthenon.

Grandparents are often the best mentors of all. They tend to care passionately about us, but are often sufficiently removed to be able to laugh when parents cannot. Because they usually have more time, they can be more available to us. Recent anthropological research suggests that grandmothers helped ensure the survival of the species by feeding their grandchildren so their daughters could give birth to more healthy children.

Grandparents are also repositories of the stories of those who went before. Our ancestors obligate us. Because they did what they did, we must do what we can do. Their stories give us courage. Toni Morrison sees her writing as a way of honoring these obligations.

> There is always an elder there. And these ancestors are not just parents, they are sort of timeless people whose relationships to the characters are benevolent, instructive, and protective, and they provide a certain kind of wisdom. . . . Whether the character was in Harlem or Arkansas, the timelessness was there, in this person who represented the ancestor. . . . When you kill the ancestor, you kill yourself.

Alex Haley puts it another way in remembering an old African saying: "Every time an old person dies, it is as if a library had burned to the ground."

In its archaic sense the word *generosity* meant "noble or highborn." It came later to mean what it means to us: "magnanimity, liberality of spirit." In either case it has the same root, *genus,* as the Latin word for family. Genealogy comes from it too. Perhaps, after all, it is family that enables us to be generous with the world and in the world. Perhaps for us to be faithful workers for the world means taking our place in the generations of our family.

We remember and tell our stories because we take courage from them. Some of the stories come from far back, from the experiences shared by our people as a whole. Some come more recently from the dangers and ordeals we ourselves have survived. The courage we have earned from what we have endured can help to carry us through. Aristotle was wrong about many things but he was right about this: courage is a habit. People are not born brave, but they become brave by doing brave things that require courage and by gleaning from those models of courage who have gone before.

At an exhibit of women artists, one of the artists left a pad of blank paper and a stack of pencils under her painting. She asked each visitor to write her genealogy on her mother's side as far back as she could. I wrote, "I am Susan, daughter of Lucile, daughter of Harriet, daughter of Nancy." I could go back no further, but those names gave me courage and made me feel strong and blessed.

I had two great-grandparents, one on my mother's side and one on my father's, who still influence my life. During a controversy at my university described later in these pages, I felt in particular need of the sustenance of forebears. I thought often in those days of the stories I had heard about my great-grandfather. As a little boy after the Civil War, he walked behind a covered wagon from Georgia to Texas to start a new life with his family. I figured if he could make it, so could I.

My friend Celeste Jones, whom I first knew as a student at Fisk University, told a related story. After the same war, her great-grandmother walked from Atlanta to Memphis to New Orleans and back to Atlanta. Along the way she collected her children who had been sold into slavery so that she might bring her family together again.

I knew my great-grandmother Helen Cline and thought of her as a friend. She died on my fifth birthday, but not before she taught me to crochet, love flowers, and not be afraid of very much, as she was not. As a child at the age of six, she hid under blankets when the Yankees came into her house after killing her uncle at the door of their home in the Shenandoah

Valley of Virginia. I know Mama Cline died with a strong feeling about Yankees, but I doubt if that feeling was fear.

We gather strength from the names of those who will not let us go, who know the difference between chaining a soul and holding a hand. These are the people in our lives who hand us a signed blank check, letting us know in their love for us that nothing we ever do could make it unredeemable.

Having a past is to possess a blessing. It is a blessing because our past, no matter how happy or hurtful, is uniquely our own. No one, not even those closest to us, has been shaped and made by it exactly as we have been. It is a blessing to have a place to come from. Nothing is lost. The past also is a blessing because, paradoxically, it is always being transformed. Those who have peopled our past change and grow as we change and grow.

Our past can see us through. I spend a good deal of time reading and thinking and writing about the *Aeneid*, the epic of the founding of Rome by the great poet Vergil. Its hero, Aeneas, shipwrecked and desperately homeless at the beginning of the poem, has been a boat person already for seven years, forbidden to settle on every shore he has reached. Even in those circumstances he is able to say to his band of fellow survivors: "We have suffered worse things than this in the past; we can endure this too. And perhaps someday it will be pleasing to remember even these things."

Nikos Kazantzakis understands this poignantly in *The Saviors of God:* "The cry is not yours. It is not you talking, but innumerable ancestors talking with your mouth. It is not you who desire, but innumerable generations of descendants longing with your heart." We are all the product of at least five generations. When we speak, we are speaking not only our words but the words also of our ancestors.

At the same time, we are the repositories of the hopes and aspirations of the next generations. We are placed at a post of responsibility in the chain of the generations. Kazantzakis continues: "And our ancestors are always crying: Finish our work, finish our work!"

The documentary of Martin Luther King's mission, *From Montgomery to Memphis*, contains the unspoken refrain, "Finish our work, finish our work!" That cry began long before King cried it. All day and all night his ancestors and ours come and cry out, in Kazantzakis's words, "No, we have not gone. We have not detached ourselves from you. We have not descended into the earth. Deep in your entrails we continue the struggle. Deliver us!"

Kazantzakis would say that we are giving birth not only to the future but also to the previous generations, to those hopes and dreams that brought us as far as we are. He says, "You have a great responsibility. You do not govern now only your own small, insignificant existence. You are a throw of the dice on which, for a moment, the entire fate of your race is gambled."

4

WHEN THE YOUNG POINT THE WAY

At the same time, Odysseus set off toward the city. Pallas Athena, harboring kindness for the hero, drifted a heavy mist around him, shielding him from any swaggering islander who'd cross his path, provoke him with taunts and search out who he was. Instead, as he was about to enter the welcome city, the bright-eyed goddess herself came up to greet him there, for all the world like a young girl, holding a pitcher, standing face-to-face with the visitor, who asked, "Little girl, now wouldn't you be my guide to the palace of the one they call Alcinous? The king who rules the people of these parts. I am a stranger, you see, weighed down with troubles, come this way from a distant, far-off shore. So I know no one here, none at all in your city and the farmlands round about."

"Oh yes, sir, good old stranger," the bright-eyed goddess said, "I'll show you the very palace that you're after—the king lives right beside my noble father. Come quietly, too, and I will lead the way."

. . . .

And Pallas Athena sped away in the lead as he followed in her footsteps, man and goddess. But the famed Phaeacian sailors never saw him, right in their midst, striding down their streets. Athena the one with lovely braids would not permit it.

Odyssey 7.14–33, 42–46

A young girl, carrying a pitcher, meets Odysseus in the streets of Phaeacia where he has drifted onto the shore. Athena, in the form of the friend of Princess Nausicaa, contrived to ensure his safe initial reception, but now Odysseus must be protected through the city en route to the palace of the local king, Alcinous. A mist provided by Athena covers the hero's approach, but it is a child in pigtails who appears to lead him where he needs to go. Phaeacia is not noticeably a hospitable land, so Odysseus' future depends on this protection and guidance.

It matters that the child is holding a pitcher in her hands. Even children, heartbreakingly, have learned to carry weapons in modern regions torn by war. If something benign is held in one's hands, however, harm is less likely and a newcomer's sense of safety is increased.

In this scene Athena appears as a child who leads the way. A certain delicacy is required in discussing children as mentors. For many, sentimentality in the case of children is almost unavoidable. They are so innocent, so "new from God," that we may be inclined to grant them greater credence than we should. Children are capable also of great cruelty, especially to one another. *The Lord of the Flies* is not an exaggeration.

For at least three reasons, however, children belong in a discussion of mentors as surely as Athena-as-girlchild belongs in the *Odyssey*. First, children are the great observers, often

seeing things about adults that are harder for us to see in ourselves. Second, they have not yet been fully schooled in the
social codes that prescribe words and thought. Finally, if they
have been at all nurtured, they are less honed by hard living
and humbled by the human condition than are the adults
around them. As a result, their imaginations are vividly capable of making uncommon connections.

For some children the highly imaginative years of childhood are prolonged because of illness. Two of the finest writers I know suffered that experience, and both say that the best
thing that can happen to a writer is an extended illness in
childhood. Given few outlets except reading—and no television, which seems to be a defining factor for creativity—their
imagination nourishes itself.

The children we know can point the way. On one occasion
a four-year-old child and I climbed a high pasture at our farm
to search out the remains of a mother cow we had pulled over
to the tree line a month earlier after she died while calving.
For a while we sat quietly by the bleached bones. Then with
no preface the boy said, "There are no grown-ups. There are
only grown-bigs. God is the only grown-up."

I do not know the source of that observation. Nor can I
trace the origins of a dinner-table reflection of a little girl at
about the same age: "I know who the president of the world
is. It's God. And we did not elect God. God elected us."

For years and years I did not think I could write a book.
Given the limiting perceptions about gender I had observed
and absorbed, I assumed that only men produced serious
scholarship. I enjoyed writing articles, however, especially
about Vergil's *Aeneid*. One day out of curiosity I arranged
those articles around the dining room table. Our daughter
wandered into the room, took one look, and said, "Mom, if
you put all that together, you would have a book." That moment gave birth to my realization that I *could* write a book, a

notion that for years had seemed as illusionary to me as playing dress-up in my mother's clothes. I was forty-eight years old when my first book was published.

Elizabeth Cady Stanton firmly proclaimed, "I shall not grow conservative with age." Once when I was especially tired from whatever I was doing at the time, I muttered to my young children, "Maybe I *will* grow conservative with age. I'm not sure I can keep this up." Upon hearing my complaint they remonstrated, "If you do that, we will not cook for you when we grow up, we will not come to visit you, and we will not even talk to you on the telephone." The young people break the bones in our heads so we can continue to grow. It is their great gift.

The four children of a friend of mine were still quite young when my friend was offered a job that would have more than doubled his salary. He was struggling to make ends meet, and the offer was tempting. The new job meant, however, that he would leave home early on Monday morning and return Friday night or Saturday. He talked first with his wife about it, then the two of them summoned a family council. The three older children had many things to say. The youngest son sat quietly. Finally he asked, "Dad, if you take that job, who will put up the tent?" The conversation was over. The father cried. He kept his old job, and the family enjoyed many more years of camping together.

The children we learn from do not have to be our own. A young woman without children told me about the importance to her of her four-year-old niece. "She makes me want to be a better person," said my friend, "so I can be a better influence on her."

At a picnic while still in graduate school, I met a family from India whose eleven-year-old daughter seemed unusually conversant and forthcoming with adults. When I commented to her that she did not seem to be shy, she replied, "Why should I be shy? If I were, I would miss out on learning many new things."

Children who enjoy the company of adults are reaching for their full humanity. The challenge for adults is to allow and encourage such relationships. Jesus' disciples were early of-fenders here. They thought it would be a waste of time for Jesus to pay attention to the children who had been brought to him. Jesus had to set them straight: "Let the children come to me; do not try to stop them; for the kingdom of Heaven be-longs to such as these."

Our much-loved children start leaving us as soon as they are born. It is a good thing they do. As William Sloan Coffin points out, if that were not the case, slavery would never have been abolished, there would have been no civil rights move-ment, no women's movement, no gay rights movement, no movement for a nonnuclear future. It is a good thing that our children leave us, he continues, because if they did not, there would be no hope for making things better in the world.

From one of my students I had learned the truth of Coffin's remark well before I heard it from Coffin. The student was a young man from Houston in my freshman seminar who had sat quietly in the rear of the room until we came to a discus-sion of Aristotle. In the *Nichomachaean Ethics*, Aristotle pro-poses that parents love their children more than children love their parents. I asked the class, young men and women who had left their homes for college only weeks before, if they thought this were true. Forest volunteered immediately: "Yes, Aristotle is right. Our parents *do* love us more than we love them. And it is a good thing they do, because change in the world requires risk and struggle—and what our parents want most for us is to be safe."

When our children leave us, it may be for college or for work we do not know or for other ways of life to which we are unaccustomed. In his hymn "Oh God Who to a Loyal Home,"

Harry Emerson Fosdick urges the case for peaceful homes as places of nurturance. Nevertheless, he recognizes that our homes can become bastions against the world if they are not connected to work for the sake of the world outside. Fosdick affirms the ultimate purpose of peaceful homes:

> Oh God of life, send from above
> Thy succor, swift and strong,
> That from such homes stout souls may come
> To triumph over wrong.

Understood in this way, our homes are places of nurture but also of preparation. From such places some stalwart souls will envision the world in new ways. That process is by no means an easy one.

One of my friends is convinced that the most subversive lyrics of any song sung by our generation of Protestant children growing up in the South were these:

> Jesus loves the little children,
> All the children of the world,
> Red and yellow, black and white:
> They are precious in his sight.
> Jesus loves the little children of the world.

Wayne sang these words as a child in Sunday school. His mother taught the song in vacation Bible school until the elders in that South Carolina community instructed her not to. But it was too late. My friend already believed them. As he grew older, he saw the immense disconnect between the lyrics and the life he was living under segregation. More than that, he saw the disconnect between what he was living and almost everything else he was being taught by the church. There was nothing for him to do but to try to make the world conform to the beliefs he learned when he was little.

As a college student, Wayne was active in efforts to end the practices of racial segregation at his university. As a young field manager for a major national corporation he broke all precedent, successfully, by hiring African American women as truck drivers. Later he worked in political campaigns motivated by the same values. Today as a businessman he engages in fair hiring policies. He is still an activist and a believer in those subversive lyrics he sang as a child. He and his wife chose to join a United Methodist congregation in which they are the only white members.

Our children, our families, our close communities obligate us to finish the work of the past and to continue the work of the future. The moral imagination of children sometimes points the way.

The medieval monk Bernard of Clairvaux said that we must be not like channels but like reservoirs, which receive, store up, then give from their excess. Our place in the generations is like that. We receive strength from those who went before. We store up, reshape, then send out. If we are only channels, if we are only insignificant moments in a meaningless passage of time, we can run dry.

Our children, all our children, obligate us never to run dry. Their gifts to us help ensure that we do not.

5

THE SAVING
GRACE OF ART

*But now Athena appeared and came toward him. She looked like
a young man . . . a shepherd boy yet elegant too, with all the gifts
that grace the sons of kings, with a well-cut cloak falling in folds
across her shoulders, sandals under her shining feet, a hunting spear
in hand.*

Odyssey 13.252–56

Odysseus is in great danger when he is brought
home to Ithaca by the Phaeacians. He cannot
simply walk into the palace and announce that he
is home. The situation with the suitors is far too dangerous.
When he awakes from his sleep under an olive tree, he does
not even know where he is. The first person he sees is a young
shepherd, who assures him that he is home in his native land.
Upon hearing this, Odysseus laughs, knowing that he is hearing Ithaca described by Pallas Athena. He answers with a long
lying tale, saying that he is a refugee from Crete, testing
Athena in the same way that she tested him.

*As his story ended, goddess Athena, gray eyes gleaming, broke into
a smile and stroked him with her hand, and now she appeared a
woman, beautiful, tall and skilled at weaving lovely things. Her
words went flying straight toward Odysseus: "Any man—any god
who met you—would have to be some champion lying cheat to get
past you for all-round craft and guile! You terrible man, foxy, in-
genious, never tired of twists and tricks—so, not even here, on native soil, would you give up those wily tales that warm the cockles
of your heart! Come, enough of this now. We're both old hands at
the arts of intrigue. Here among mortal men you're far the best at
tactics, spinning yarns, and I am famous among the gods for wisdom, cunning wiles, too."*

Odyssey 13.324–39

Then goddess and hero turn to plotting against the suitors
who have occupied Odysseus's palace for years—pursuing
Penelope's hand in marriage, bullying the household staff, in-
timidating the young man of the family, and feasting daily on
the master's flocks.

In this scene a playful ease marks the relationship between
Odysseus and Athena. They spark each other's repartee, and
their laughter affirms their comradery. Athena seems almost
a peer, the right companion in the right place at the right
time.

Most of all, both god and mortal are conspicuous here
as performing artists. The performance mode is apt because
the *Iliad* and *Odyssey* originated in oral performance.
Something—we do not know what—happened at Troy, called
Ilium by the ancient Greeks, sometime in the twelfth century
B.C.E. (For literalists, tradition dates the fall of Troy to August 18, 1185 B.C.E.) Those events gave rise to stories that in
time were taken up by wandering bards, who elaborated them

over a period of more than four hundred years and sang them at the great religious festivals. Not long after writing was introduced to Greece, the two epics were written down, perhaps given their final shaping by a poet named Homer and dictated by him to a literate scribe sometime between 750 and 725 B.C.E.

We learned more about how all this may have happened from a scholar named Milman Parry who studied long oral poems still being performed in the 1930s by illiterate Croatian bards. These Croatian performers did not memorize their poems but pieced stories together as they performed them for entertainment. Parry concluded that the oral composition of the Homeric epics may have occurred in a similar way.

The entire *Odyssey* is thus a performance piece, and Athena is the finest performer of all. She is an actor and a mime, a master of disguise, variously male or female, young or old. She is the magician of metamorphosis, slipping through keyholes or swooping up to the rafters as a swallow. She is the laughing, gray-eyed goddess who seems to relish her roles. For his part, Odysseus, within the confines of his mortality, is a man of as many turns as she.

Artists are the mentors of our imagination. Without them, we would be poor creatures indeed, slumping sullenly from sleep to food to work to food and back to sleep again. The arts—painting, sculpture, music, dance, theater, the written word in its forms—not only enhance life, they *are* life. They add flesh to the curves and colors and leaps of spirit that make us truly human.

Artists as Mentors

In almost every room of my home is a work of art by Mona Pierce. A casual observer might not notice, because in over six decades of making art, Mona never repeated herself. Other Texas artists painted bluebonnets. Mona hammered copper, etched silver, carved wood, and painted with oils, watercolor, and acrylics. At the end of her life she was still experimenting with new forms of texture and collage.

Mona lived next door the whole time I was growing up. Because of her, my first ambition was to be an artist. Probably my original fascination was that she had a place of her own to work—first a converted garage, then a separate studio built for that purpose in her backyard. Her stacks of canvases and paints and copper and glass and tiles and brushes and palettes seemed to me a vast treasure trove, a glimmering, mysterious magnet.

Mona was like no other woman I knew in my still circumscribed world. In the world of females I inhabited, cheerful good manners, strewn more or less indiscriminately, mattered supremely. That is the charm of traditional female Southern culture, of course, and also the implacable code that exacts conformity. I sense in retrospect that what I found so entrancing about Mona was her focus.

Mona did not try to be different. She simply *was* different because the rest of her trailed along behind her focus. She was completely self-taught, although she often attended workshops and both entered and judged competitions. When she married at eighteen, she had the good luck or good judgment to marry the right man. Her two daughters, especially the oldest, were also creative, and one of her grandsons is a famous silversmith.

In my household, abstinence from alcohol was practiced and piety was prized. Mona Pierce drank Scotch whisky every evening. She did not go to church. She wore colorful clothes. She and her husband George built the only two-story New England-style house in our Lubbock neighborhood of conventional one-story ranch-style dwellings. They did not put

up their Christmas tree until Christmas Eve, three weeks after everyone else. Even more remarkable to me in that time
and place, George manifestly supported Mona in her work
and helped her with it constantly in such material ways as
building frames and soldering metal.

Mona traveled for the sake of art to the Southwest, Mexico, down into the catacombs of Rome. She could be repre-
sentational or abstract. She had a stunning sense of color and
design. Her vast knowledge of religious iconography led to a
commission from a local Episcopal church for an exquisite series of the Twelve Apostles in enamel on copper.

I spent as much time in Mona's studio as I could. She never
treated me as a child or guest. Rather, she extended the greater
gift of taking my presence for granted. I would watch her for
hours, especially intrigued with her beautiful mosaics. Once
she let me help lay the mosaic border around a circular enamel
piece of the Virgin Mary. I placed a gold tile out of sequence,
clearly in the wrong place. Mona did not correct my mistake.
I wonder now if she even noticed it. Asymmetry did not
bother her, and her ease with disorder made a lasting impression on me.

Mona seldom talked about her art. Once she commented,
however, "I do with art what you and your mother and Mary
Louise do with words."

While I was in graduate school in New York, Mona came
to New Jersey to visit one of her daughters. Then she came
to visit me, and we spent a day together in Manhattan going
to museums. At the newly opened Whitney, she stopped at
the entrance to each gallery and named the artist of each
painting in the room. I was amazed. What I had not known
during my childhood was that while Mona was making art
during the day, she was also reading about it late into the
night.

Mona was a companion. When I defended my dissertation

on Boethius at the end of my time at Columbia in 1967, I was asked to write an additional chapter. That led to my decision to rewrite the whole thesis. I went home to Texas that summer to complete the writing before I was to begin teaching at the University of Illinois in the fall. By that time we had built a small guest house in our backyard, just across the fence from Mona's studio. That is where I wrote and slept.

Surely I did not work twenty hours a day, but that is my memory of it. All my waking hours except Monday nights at 7:00, when I went into the house to watch Ben Gazarra's wonderful series "Run for Your Life," I was closeted in the guest house struggling with Boethius. It was a lonely struggle.

That entire summer, however, it seemed to me as I would look across the back fence late at night that Mona never turned off the light in her studio before I turned off mine.

I know more about how my friend and Nashville neighbor Bill Myers became an artist because I asked both him and his parents about it. Bill started drawing at two. When he was three, his parents took him to visit a nearby fire station. Upon returning home, he drew the fire engine, from memory, in perfect detail. His mother and father recognized his gift at that moment and thereafter never failed to support it.

Bill was the first-born of three children. His parents never told him he could not make a living as an artist; they figured he knew what he was doing. When he was seven or eight, his family moved to the city where the state university is located. Since no one there offered art classes for children, his parents arranged for Bill to study in a college art class with the "adults." The class had a nude female model, which Bill laughingly says determined his career in art. His course, however, was already settled. He never knew anything else, and no one with power over his life bothered to tell him that he could not do what he loved for a living.

Bill recalls that his parents did not spend much time praising him. Instead, they gave him something far better than praise: a steady supply of paper and pencils. Born in 1940, Bill did not have white paper for drawing until World War II was over, only the yellowish manila kind. When the white paper appeared, it was, he says, "dreamy." His mother recalls buying Bill a five-dollar watercolor brush he asked for when he was still a young child. Her tone and smile registered both the cost to the family of the brush and her respect for the child who asked for it.

On the matter of praise, Bill advises parents who consult with him about their children to offer it sparingly. Or rather, not to toss off verbal praise but rather to provide the substantive means for children to pursue their interests and talents, even if it means rearranging a family's life around them. When praise from parents is words only, he cautions, children learn quickly not to believe them.

Another creative friend had the opposite experience of being dismissed by a parent. Nella tells of going to a ballet at the age of eleven. When she returned, she made a painting of it. Her mother said, "Oh, Nella, your pictures are lovely, but they are accidents." Nella was crushed. She took her painting and her heartbreak to Mrs. Kimbrough, her art teacher in the New York City public art and music school Nella attended. Mrs. Kimbrough laughed. "Nella," she said, "all art is an accident."

The laughter saved the child. After a forty-eight-year hiatus as a physician, Nella has now returned to her art with more passion than ever before.

At the age of seventy-five, composer Ned Rorem said, "I'm very lucky to have always known what I wanted to do. Not many people can say the same. That goes for Donald Trump, who is a billionaire because he couldn't do anything else. Artists, who are thought so crazy, are the most stable people in the world, because they know what they must do all their lives."

Millard Sheets was a leading watercolorist, acclaimed designer of art for public spaces, and a man whose large-hearted love of the world embraced all who met him. Millard belied the stereotype of artist as recluse or misanthrope. His passion to "bring art to the people" took its most public form in commissions such as his dome mosaic for the National Shrine of the Immaculate Conception in Washington, D.C., and the award-winning 60-by-22-foot mural in the portico of the Detroit Public Library. Our teenaged son Matthew, however, was most smitten to meet the artist of what football fans call "Touchdown Jesus" and the rest of us know as the soaring mural on the facade of the University of Notre Dame Library tower. The 134-by-68-foot mural, made of mosaic pieces from 143 shades of granite, portrays Jesus with upraised arms, a host of disciples and scholars marshalled around him.

While Millard was in my hometown preparing a large mural for the new civic auditorium, my mother invited him for dinner. Happily I was home for a visit, and the two of us slipped away to the living room for a conversation that took off instantly and flew straight to the mark of what seemed to matter most to us both. When we returned to the kitchen, Millard reported, "Susan and I just talked for three weeks in twenty minutes."

I remember he told me how he had gone straight from high school in California to art school, much to the dismay of his father. He told me about a professor he admired who said to him archly that he had to be truly educated if he wanted to be an artist. Angry at first, then deeply chastened, Millard was standing outside the professor's office when he arrived early the next morning. "Please tell me how to go about getting

educated," he begged. Millard's education in history, literature, and philosophy began that day.

The lessons took. As he reflected later, "To become an
artist, one must become a total person. The broader the base
of general education, the more able the artist is to cope with
the environment. I believe too that gratitude for life itself is
basic to the development of insight beyond the average."

A day or two after our conversation, I attended a lecture
Millard gave at the local university. Millard spoke of art as
a tripartite activity. The first part, he said, is to learn the
language, to acquire the skills necessary for our work. The
second is to bring everything we know from the life we have
lived to the work that we do. The third and final part is to
build bridges back to the world, to give to the world in our
own voice the stories we bring to the language we have
learned.

What we learn from artists is transferrable. The notion of
art as a tripartite activity applies to any form of creativity, as I
came eventually to see in the case of Buddy Holly.

I did not grow up with the music.

In fact, as a teenager in the 1950s in Lubbock, Texas, I
avoided popular music with the same perverse snobbery that
in elementary school caused me to wear the collars of my
Ship 'n' Shore blouses turned down in back as flat as my
chest was in front—the collars that most of my schoolmates
turned up, seductively they must have thought, behind their
necks.

I thus stepped way out of my self-consciously studious world
on the afternoon of June 3, 1955, when I went downtown with
some of my friends to see a singer they had heard about perform
at the newly opened body shop of the Johnson-Connelly Pon-
tiac dealership.

When we arrived, three scrawny boys were leaning against

the far wall, guitars in tow. Eventually a pink Cadillac with the top down drove in through the open bay door. The scrawny boys played for a little while. Then the passenger in the front seat of the Cadillac stepped out, wordlessly hoisted his guitar over his orange jacket, purple t-shirt, and red slacks, and started singing and playing.

True to form, I disdained the whole proceeding, especially the screams and giggles from the audience. I stood aloof at the back of the room, ponytail resolutely still, glad that no one besides my friends noticed I was there.

It took me twelve more years of education, four years of living in New York City, and twenty-five more years of growing up to figure out the significance of Buddy Holly, the warm-up act for Elvis Presley that shiny afternoon in Lubbock.

Fast forward to Champaign-Urbana, Illinois, fall of 1967. A newly minted Ph.D. has just finished teaching the first class of her career—ever. Not even a teaching assistantship along the way. All of her students must have known it right away, but one had the poise afterwards to ask, "Miss Ford, I may be wrong, but I wonder if this is the first class you have ever taught?" "How did you guess?" I gasped. Kindly he said, "I have a book that might help you."

The next class meeting he brought me *Teacher* by Sylvia Ashton-Warner, in which the author describes teaching young aboriginal children in New Zealand. Ashton-Warner soon discarded the standard British texts with which she had been provided. Instead, she asked the children to tell her the stories they had heard growing up in their Maori communities. She wrote them down, and from their own stories she taught these five-year-old children to read.

For the past thirty years I have taught Latin, Greek, and classical civilization to college students. Ashton-Warner's example of using what we grew up with to help us learn continues to be the best teacher training I have ever had.

Still, it took me a very long time to put my beliefs into practice in my own writing and scholarship, especially in front of my peers. I was helped on that journey by John Goldrosen's 1979 biography, *The Buddy Holly Story*. When I read about the influences on Holly, something clicked.

In the spring of 1980, in Columbia, South Carolina, at a meeting of the Classical Association of the Middle West and South, I took the risk. I was scheduled that afternoon to talk about the *Aeneid* and why it was a permanent achievement that far surpassed its own time and place of first-century B.C. Rome. I proposed that Vergil took in everything around him from his rural Italian origins, practiced profoundly the skills of the poet's trade, then married those gifts to a tradition he appropriated from far away: the *Iliad* and the *Odyssey* from Homer's Greece.

Then I paused, took a deep breath, and took the leap.

"It's what Buddy Holly did," I said. "He took in all that country music he grew up with around Lubbock, Texas, he practiced his music all the time, then he crawled into his daddy's car late at night to listen to radio broadcasts of black music from Louisiana. He put it all together, and that's how he helped invent rock 'n' roll."

Having never heard any of my scholarly colleagues say anything as down-home as this, I sat down right away. When I looked up anxiously, I was surrounded by a crowd, a veritable gaggle of bald heads, old, respectable bald heads—all of them raving about Buddy Holly.

"I've been a Holly fan all my life," said one, whose years made the literal statement impossible. Said another: "I made a pilgrimage all the way from Saskatchewan to Lubbock, Texas, to visit Buddy Holly's grave." "Are you really from Lubbock?" asked a third, wide-eyed. I smiled demurely.

In that moment I came to understand the full measure of Buddy Holly's creativity: the courage to honor one's legacy, hone the required skills, then gather into it the unknown, untried, and strange in order to invent something new.

Buddy Holly had the careless courage of assuming that there was simply not anything he could not do. I don't know which example of his grinning gumption I admire more: his asking his parents to invite the outrageous Little Richard home for dinner (they finally compromised on a backyard barbecue, probably the first integrated outdoor social occasion in Lubbock) or his request of his brother Larry for a thousand dollars.

Philip Norman reports the conversation between Buddy and his oldest brother, Larry, the one who knew him best, as recounted by Larry himself:

> He came to me and said, "Larry, I know good and well I could make it if only I had me a decent guitar and some decent clothes." I said, "Make it as what?" He said, "Why, make it in the music business." So I said, "Okay, how much do you need?," thinking he was going to say about fifty dollars. But Buddy says, "How about lending me a thousand dollars?"
>
> Well, I was pretty amazed, because that was a pile of money back then, but I reckoned he knew what he was about, so I scraped up the thousand bucks from somewhere.

At the time of the unveiling of the Buddy Holly statue at the new Civic Center in Lubbock, Ed Ward, a reporter from Austin, came up to Lubbock with a friend, a Lubbock native whom Ward identified only as Joe Bob, to tour the town. On the way back to Austin, Ward asked his friend to explain why so much rock 'n' roll energy came from Lubbock. Joe Bob answered, "If you don't play football and your life isn't consumed by Jesus, what else is there to do but drink beer and ride the Loop, or, if you're like Buddy and you don't drink, sit home and dream that your guitar is gonna get you out some day?"

Joe Bob may have been right, except for the last part.

I'll take another try at it. I propose that Buddy Holly

achieved what he did also because he was happy. What I mean by happy is that he was secure. He was secure first because his family always encouraged him and thought his music was a fine thing for him to be doing. That kind of security made Holly free to be generous and loyal to his friends and to his hometown, including Tabernacle Baptist Church. It made him know too that his music could make a place for him wherever he was, whether at the J. T. Hutchinson Junior High parents' appreciation night or in New York City at the Apollo Theater in Harlem.

Because Holly was secure, he was also hospitable, and not just to Little Richard. His friend Peggy Sue Gerron recalls: "Buddy Holley always said, 'I'm from Lubbock, Texas'. . . . When Buddy carried that West Texas hospitality out into the world, he made the world want to come visit his hometown." (On his first recording contract, Buddy's last name was misspelled "Holly" and stayed that way.)

There is more than one way to be an artist—as many ways as there are artists, because that's what art is. But it is not true that one has to be anguished to make a poem or a painting or anything else.

When you are secure, you are also free to write your music out of what you know. Buddy Holly always did that, which is why his songs still resonate with authenticity. When you are happy, you don't have to leave your home and family to seek out some anonymous city. Nor do you have to turn your back on the values with which you were raised. Goldrosen writes that Holly was "fresh and new, but still lived by old rules of ambition and achievement." Holly was raised to work hard, and he never quit. He never repeated himself either. When he died in a plane crash in 1959 at the age of twenty-two, he had recorded over fifty songs of astonishing variety and had written many of them.

My scholarly colleagues in South Carolina that afternoon

had to ask me the question, of course: "Did you *know* him?" I had to answer "No."

I might have met him, it turns out, because Holly used to play at our house on 21st Street with my older brother Davis—his 1955 classmate at Lubbock High—but that ended in junior high when my football-playing brother decided Buddy wasn't cool because he played music instead of sports.

I know Buddy Holly now. Unlike Holly, however, who did not have to leave Lubbock to learn it, I had to journey far and long to figure out the marriage of familiar and strange that is the essence of creativity.

I now know also what T. S. Eliot meant when he said that we never cease our exploration, so that some day we may return home and know the place for the first time.

Performers as Guides

I suspect that most of my attachment to Buddy Holly lies more in respect for his creativity and in regional loyalty than in my own ear for music. I know for a fact that the performing art in which I delight most is theater.

Drama is in my bones. We are all born into a major production, each with its unique cast of characters and a script always in progress. Why I took to heart and mind the drama of my particular family, both as critic and participant, when my two older siblings did not, I do not know. In college I learned to love the great Greek plays. On my first trip to Greece I saw a performance of Euripides' *Hecuba* at the theater in Epidauros. Later in New York, when I discovered that even a graduate student could afford standing room at Wednesday matinees, all those rapt afternoons in darkened theaters seemed to me like bountiful homecomings.

Laurence Olivier claimed that he began creating any character he was to perform by imagining that person as a painting.

"To create a character, I first visualize a painting; the manner, movement, gestures, walk all follow. . . . Pictures and sounds begin to form in my mind, subconsciously at first, but slowly working their way to the surface. You keep the image in the heart and then project it onto the oil painting. I say 'oil' rather than 'watercolor' because for me, acting will always be in oils." Olivier said that he developed his Lear from Rembrandt's *Jeremiah Lamenting the Destruction of Jerusalem*.

Like most artists who win our hearts, Olivier spoke of the joy of his work. Even of his massive task of transposing *Hamlet* to film, as he did in the 1948 version in which he starred as well as directed, he acknowledged the joy: "If the shooting has been successful, editing a film is the pinnacle of a director's joy; if not, he must make it so, with no regrets about what exists or does not exist on film, because it's only his joy which will transform the lengths of film and sound track into the realization of his imagination."

Joy is closely joined with love. Even Olivier sometimes suffered from the critics, especially when he took on roles considered wrong for or beneath him. In response he wrote, "Sometimes I think that more critics should be encouraged to sit in on rehearsals so that they could see the amount of work, concentration, belief and love that goes into the construction of a piece, before they take their inky swords to it."

Love for one's work engenders obligation to one's audience. The great actress Lillian Gish put it this way: "An audience is entitled to the best performance you can give. Nothing in your personal life must interfere, neither fatigue, illness, nor anxiety—not even joy." Alexandra Danilova, star of the Ballet Russe in the forties and fifties, believed that no audience was too small or mean to merit one's best: "I never danced for an audience that I thought was unworthy of my performance." In her autobiography she wrote, "Every woman has an image—mother, princess, ballerina—that she must uphold. I was privileged to be a ballerina and I, therefore, had a duty to my audience."

As I saw firsthand with Millard Sheets, Laurence Olivier's joy and love lasted his lifetime. "I am seventeen going on eighty," he wrote in 1986. "I will continue to learn until all ceases to function. I know that the earth turns and that the sun sets and the sun rises, but I must always remember that somewhere in the shadows there are new things to be seen."

This same wonderment, this child's joy in creating, marked the life and work of Nikos Kazantzakis. At the age of 63 as he was writing *Freedom or Death*, Kazantzakis said: "I'm continuing to work calmly . . . and I'm happy that I've embarked upon a new genre—the novel—because with this my time passes and I believe I'm becoming rejuvenated. I'm writing it in high spirits and in a virgin manner, like a newcomer who has just now begun writing."

Olympia Dukakis demonstrated the same sort of creative passion in a master class for young actors I was invited to observe at my university. For three days I was riveted by the intensity and skill of her teaching.

"Don't talk until you've got your body and words together," she insisted. "Concentrate your way into the passion of what you already know." "The way into a play has to be deeply personal. You have a script here, but you must personalize it, make it your own." "Let the little things happen." "Give up every other action except the one you are doing right now." "Take the thought and let it have its way with you." "Claim these stories for yourselves. Otherwise, you're doing sketches."

Frequently I was able to translate what Dukakis said about acting to my more prosaic craft, in part because the focus of the class was on the performance of Greek drama. Dukakis herself was preparing for a performance of Euripides' *Hecuba* at the theatre of Herodes Atticus in Athens the following September.

But for conveying the passion of my stories, I have no voice, no physical body to connect with the words, no timing or technique to hone. I have at my disposal only those twenty-six limber little acrobats of the alphabet. I line them up over and over again, pushing them to bend and stretch and touch and reach far and wide enough to get close to what I mean, to what I yearn for, which is always more than what I already know.

I am reminded that performing a role changes us, just as writing changes us. "If we're intact, we're in trouble," said Dukakis. And finally, in that mysterious, transformative way, feelings and experiences too harrowing in life become safe on the stage, as they are safe also on the page. One of the true purposes of art is to avoid personal replication of demonic tragedy.

At the end of a contemporary New York production of *The Diary of Anne Frank*, the stage goes dark. When light returns, a passage from Anne Frank's pages is illuminated across the stage: "Only the writing remains."

An acquaintance told me about growing up in Germany where the office of her physician father was located in their home. Sigrid saw many artists and musicians coming in and out of her father's office. When she began to notice that they seemed not to be paying for their services, she asked her father about it. "Sigrid," he replied simply, "we must take care of artists."

We must take care of artists because art can save our lives. Lezley Saar, daughter of mixed-media artist Betye Saar, was determined not to follow the artistic career of her mother (and also her sister). Then her daughter was diagnosed with autism at age five. In her determination to stand close by her daughter, Lezley Saar began to create art and now holds her own one-woman shows. She thinks of art as engaging in "repetitive rituals." "It's what people do," she says, "to gain a sense of control in a random and chaotic world. I think of art-making as a repetitive ritual, one that helps keep me sane."

Artists also save our imagination. I met Madeleine L'Engle when I attended a conference she conducted at a retreat center in North Carolina. She told how her Newberry Prize-winning book, A *Wrinkle in Time*, turns up repeatedly on the lists of books certain groups seek to ban from public libraries. When she studied the lists, L'Engle said, she found that the one feature all the books have in common is imagination.

The artists who are mentors to us are those who help us see, think, and experience life in new ways. They point to the hearths where we alone lay the fire.

6

THE CHANCE
ENCOUNTER

*Up he [Odysseus] sprang, cloak and all, and seized a discus, huge
and heavy, more weighty by far than those the Phaeacians used to
hurl and test each other. Wheeling round, he let loose with his great
hand and the stone whirred on—and down to ground they went,
those lords of the long oars and master mariners cringing under the
rock's onrush, soaring lightly out of his grip, flying away past all the
other marks, and Queen Athena, built like a man, staked out the
spot and cried with a voice of triumph, "Even a blind man, friend,
could find your mark by groping round—it's not mixed up in the
crowd, it's far in front! There's nothing to fear in this event—no
one can touch you, much less beat your distance!"*

*At that the heart of the long-suffering hero laughed, so glad to
find a ready friend in the crowd.*

Odyssey 8.216–31

Once Odysseus receives hospitality in the palace
in Phaeacia, the local blades realize that their own
reputations are at stake and must be defended. Right
away they start taunting the stranger to enter into sporting
contests with them. Like swaggering challengers on any

playing field, they mean business. Is this interloper a real man? If so, can they improve their rankings by defeating him on their own turf?

His tactful reluctance overcome, Odysseus agrees to compete. He picks up a huge stone for the discus throw, one far heavier than any other used in the event, and hurls it with such force that the onlookers hit the ground at its onrush. Athena, disguised as a bystander watching the contest, marks the place and cries with a boast to Odysseus that no one even came close in this contest, so far out in front is his stone.

As the Phaeacian bystander, Athena addresses Odysseus as *xeinos*, the term that can mean "stranger" but here is the friendlier "guest." Odysseus delights to find in the crowd a kindly companion, someone on his side, after struggling alone for so long. His confidence is restored from this unforeseen source at the moment he needs it most. The bystander's announcement confirms who Odysseus really is.

Often mentoring is pickup work, a chance occurrence or remark that changes us in important ways. Our lives are not predetermined, but as full of contingency as the games of children in a park. Sometimes the persons who serve as our mentors are only acquaintances or even strangers standing by. A chance remark may help us identify or validate our vocation. It may provide insights that bring about new ways of living. The stranger at our side may lend meaning to events we have already experienced but do not understand.

The artist Marilyn Murphy grew up in a creative family. Since she was, as she says, "a good child," the nuns in her Catholic kindergarten allowed her to play with clay while the other children had to take naps. Still, she knew from her early years that she was "condemned to go to college," and she could never figure out how she could go to college and still do what she loved to do.

One day on the playground in the fourth grade, Marilyn

overheard one boy tell another that his brother majored in art in college. She still remembers the sounds around her and the texture and color of the silver paint on the basketball goal she was leaning against when she heard this remark. In that moment she knew for certain that her life would be all right: she could go to college and still be an artist. She now chairs a university department of fine arts and exhibits her paintings regularly.

Ginger Berrigan is a federal district court judge in New Orleans. As a young woman she participated in the civil rights movement throughout the South. She had many other possibilities in mind about her future until one day, almost as an aside, Charles Evers said to her, "You should go to law school."

Eudora Welty says that she became a writer because she lacked the patience for teaching. At a local summer camp when I was nine, a counselor asked me to teach the other girls one by one how to braid lanyards from four flat, narrow strips of plastic. I felt at home and happy that afternoon, even in the repetitive tasks of teaching. I had the patience for it. From that dry, hot summer afternoon inside a canvas tent on a rattlesnake-infested rim of a West Texas mesa, I knew I would be a teacher.

At that time and place, for a female to be a teacher meant to teach English in high school. During my freshman year in college, in love with learning by then, I went for an interview with one of my professors for some sort of special program. As I left, his assistant stopped me to ask if I had ever considered teaching in college. Of course I had not. From that moment forward, however, I never considered any vocation other than the one I practice today. Thank you, Mary Hirsh.

Such chance remarks bear not just on our callings but also on our practices. My respect for any kind of work done well at any level derives in part from an experience at a lunch counter in the old local airport where I stopped one day for white bean soup. My attention kept turning to a particular waitress, as she would have been called in those days. Snugly beyond middle age, she moved with alacrity, interacted with customers warmly, and seemed fully engaged in everything she was doing. As I was leaving, I commented to her that she seemed to enjoy her work. She replied, "I have been in this job for twenty-two years, and not a day goes by that I don't learn something new about it."

On another much earlier occasion, while I was in junior high school, I was getting into a 1950s Oldsmobile station wagon to go to the home of our church youth group leaders. One of the leaders, Jane Humphries, was standing on the curb holding the door open. At that moment I said to her that I did not have time to do something she had requested of me. She looked me straight in the eye and said, "There is always time to do what you really want to do." I learned that moment that priorities, not hours, determine what we have time to do. I hope since then I have never said to anyone "I'm sorry, I don't have time." Plates may be full, other commitments may have been made, schedules may conflict, but lack of time simply will not do as an excuse.

Do such moments as these come about by chance or divine intervention? I have heard them called "providential coincidences." I do not know how to explain their happening—such questions do not lie with the limits of knowledge—but I have a hunch about the process *after* they occur.

The ground must be ready when the seed is sown, even if we do not realize this at the conscious level. "When the student is ready, the teacher will come." Even if the remark is entirely unanticipated, as in my case with Jane Humphries' comment about time, it strikes a chord that is already in place.

Then we reformulate our lives around the new knowledge. After we have done so, the chance occurrence seems necessarily to have happened for a purpose. Here is an example. One day our daughter asked me, "What if there is only one man in the world for me to marry and I never meet him?"

I told her what I suspect, that there is always more than one. Then, someday, we meet a person who resonates so intensely and fully with who we are that we re-create our lives around this new relationship, this only one. At that point, only then but ever after, the bystander becomes part of our destiny.

7

FRIENDS

Straight to his house the clear-eyed Pallas went, full of plans for
great Odysseus' journey home. She made her way to the gaily
painted room where a young girl lay asleep . . . a match for the
deathless gods in build and beauty, Nausicaa, the daughter of gen-
erous King Alcinous. Two handmaids fair as the Graces slept be-
side her, flanking the two posts, with the gleaming doors closed. But
the goddess drifted through like a breath of fresh air, rushed to the
girl's bed and hovering close she spoke, in face and form like the
shipman Dymas' daughter, a girl the princess' age, and dearest to
her heart.

Odyssey 6.15–26

A thena may come as mentor in the guise of a
friend. Sometimes friends save our lives. In this
episode of the *Odyssey*, Odysseus's life is at stake.
Suffering one more shipwreck through the wrath of Poseidon,
he has survived by holding close to a piece of the wreckage
and floating to the Phaeacian shore. If he is not received well
there, he is doomed. Athena arranges his rescue by taking the

form of the best friend of the beautiful princess Nausicaa, daughter of the king and queen of the island. We do not hear the friend's name, only that she is the daughter of the ship-man Dymas, "a girl the princess' age, and dearest to her heart" (6.26). This time Athena happily engages in femi-nine wiles.

Athena as the daughter of Dymas appears to Nausicaa and chides her for leaving her clothes strewn all around when she should be preparing her hope chest. To find a husband, Nau-sicaa needs to be looking her best. Her friend offers to help wash the clothes by making a fine excursion to the washing pools at the seashore:

> Come, let's go wash these clothes at the break of day—I'll help you, lend a hand, and the work will fly! You won't stay unwed long. The noblest men in the country court you now, all Phaeacians just like you, Phaeacia-born and raised. So come, first thing in the morning press your kingly father to harness the mules and wagon for you, all to carry your sashes, dresses, glossy spreads for your bed. It's so much nicer for you to ride than go on foot. The washing pools are just too far from town."

> Odyssey 6.33-44

Because this plan takes effect, Nausicaa is present at the seashore where she comes upon the sleeping Odysseus. He awakes, and gradually wins the princess over by his courtesy, restraint, and inborn nobility. Nor is the clever Odysseus be-yond a little harmless flirtation. It could only help his case to refer to the young woman's hopes for a husband:

> And may the good gods give you all your heart desires: husband, and house, and lasting harmony too. No finer, great gift in the

world than that . . . when man and woman possess their home, two
minds, two hearts that work as one."

Odyssey 6.198–203

One might reasonably argue that Athena's disguise here as
Nausicaa's friend is meant to help Odysseus, not Nausicaa.
The *Odyssey* is a poem of many journeys, however, not only
the hero's. Here Homer tells of the movement into maturity
of a young princess. Without the goddess's encouragement in
the form of her friend, Nausicaa would never have left home
on the journey that brings her toward her adulthood, just as a
journey with the same divine guidance brought Telemachus
toward his.

Friends as Mentors

Not all friends are mentors. Some of our friends, even close
ones, are never mentors at all. But with certain others there
come moments—a word, a suggestion, an appearance at a
time when we needed them most and may not even have
known it—when our hearts are mended and the gardens
around us made green.

Such friends meet the strict criterion of Aristotle's highest
form of friendship: two good people, alike in virtue, helping
each other become better. They have each other's best interests at heart, even at cost to themselves. Sometimes that cost
might come from posing a challenge to an action or idea of
the other. Such challenges are hard to receive and harder to
give when two people hold each other's interest at heart.

Always this high kind of friendship is a gift, bestowed freely.
Because a friend is a gift, not bound by legal or political or con-
tractual obligations, the potentiality for mentoring is secure.

Dietrich Bonhoeffer had reason to know about this kind
of friendship, forged in the cauldron of moral and political

resistance to Hitler. After his arrest in 1943, he wrote "The Friend" from his Gestapo prison cell. The language of the poem is influenced by Bonhoeffer's close friendship with Eberherd Bethge, to whom the poem was sent.

. . . .

not from the heavy soil of earth
but from the spirit's choice and free desire,
needing no oath or legal bond,
is friend bestowed on friend.

Beside the cornfield that sustains us,
tilled and cared for reverently by men
sweating as they labour at their task,
and, if need be, giving their life's blood—
beside the field that gives their daily bread
men also let the lovely cornflower thrive.
No one has planted, no one watered it;
it grows, defenceless and in freedom,
and in glad confidence of life untroubled
under the open sky.

. . . .

But always to rigorous
judgment and censure
freely assenting,
man seeks, in his manhood,
not orders, not laws and peremptory dogmas,
but counsel from one who is earnest in goodness
and faithful in friendship,
making man free.

Distant or near,
in joy or in sorrow,
each in the other
sees his true helper
to brotherly freedom.

. . . .

Gifts bestowed by such steadfast companions as these come in many forms, but they have in common their unexpected, timely, and noble quality.

One such friend gave me an extraordinary gift in a time of great need. She knew that I was grieving an irreparable loss, so raw and new that sleep did not allay its demands. Nights are the hardest in any case, stripped of even slender distractions. "I wake up easily," she told me, "and I go back to sleep easily. Call me whenever you want to, in any hour of the night. It will be okay." Because I know my friend means what she says, I called her one awful night at two o'clock in the morning. I did not call her again, but because I knew I could, I never thereafter felt lonely as I lay awake in a sleeping world.

On several occasions I have been deeply moved by friends who supported me when they did not agree with what I was doing. Shortly before leaving town for a demonstration against a proposed nuclear reactor of a kind even more dangerous than usual, I found a note in my door. "I'm not sure I agree with your position on this," my friend wrote. "But you believe it, and that means you are doing the right thing. Good luck."

During a tension-laden time when my university chose to host an event arguably supportive of apartheid in South Africa, I called on a dear friend to tell her that a march of faculty members in academic regalia was being planned to protest the decision. "I'm not asking you to do anything," I said, meaning it. "But because this is important to me, I wanted you to know about it." As we gathered for the march, I looked up to see my friend quietly approaching our group, dressed in her academic cap and gown.

Another friend, an outstanding journalist for a number of years, eventually discerned that her vocation was to the ministry. She resigned her job at the local newspaper. Her plans to attend an Episcopal seminary were all set when the school's financial situation changed, leading the school to notify my friend that she would not be receiving the fellowship it had promised.

It was like a death. My friend found another, lesser job in journalism and set about reconstituting her life in the absence of her dream. The day before she was to have started her classes, she received a Federal Express package with a letter from one of her close friends from college. Her friend wrote of the conversation she had with her husband on a hike earlier in the day. They said they could not understand why she wanted to go to seminary, since they did not believe in God. They did, however, believe in their friend.

Enclosed in the letter was a check for five thousand dollars. The note added, "This is not a loan. It is a gift." My friend began classes the following day. Now she is an ordained Episcopal priest with a parish of her own.

While teaching at the University of Illinois, I was befriended by three young women—two students and a staff member of a Methodist church—who nurtured me in our shared concerns and then helped launch me to marriage in Bangkok and a new life with Ashley Wiltshire in Nashville. One of them collaborated with me in the translation of Bonhoeffer's prison poems, including "The Friend." She is now a corporate lawyer in Chicago with Amoco. The second teaches fifth grade in Cincinnati. The third, a Chicago native and great activist, married a Southern farmer (to her surprise) and is an IRS agent in Albany, Georgia.

The four of us had not been together for thirty years when we met in Chicago for two days. The quality of our friendship became evident when we had little to say about the past and much to share about where we are now and what is important to us for the future. I realized how greatly I continue to be influenced by these women individually and as a group:

Evolution

The oak is in the acorn, they say of trees
But not of me, whose botany
assumes unprecedented lineaments
in the company of friends.

Sometimes friends who are mentors share the gift of good talk, the kind of talk that leaves both persons changed. My colleague Franklin Brooks and I began to exchange thoughts on the matter of broken hearts. We smiled about those cheap gold-tone hearts of our adolescent days in Texas, the kind that are divided into two parts by a jagged cut and worn on chains by young lovers. I said to him I thought broken hearts might be more hospitable, since they have more surfaces exposed to receive the hurts of others. When a biscuit is broken in two, it can be spread with more butter and jam.

The following day Franklin wrote me this letter:

Dear Friend,
"To break," "breaking," "broken"—these are awful words, with dreadful associations like "worthless," "useless," "devalued," "untouchable." What suffering is evoked by "broken promises," "broken bones," "a breaking heart." You were brave to hold a breaking heart in your hands, until the fear had gone away and you could see what it is like. Your thoughts encouraged me to look at breakage myself, and here is what I have seen.

"Christ, Be known to us in the breaking of the bread." The moment in the Christian mass that fills me with the deepest awe is the "fracture," when the celebrant holds the host up high, for all to see, and then breaks it in half. Our silence is profound at that dramatic moment and I am always surprised at how easy it is to hear the crack as the wafer breaks, throughout the church. Such a little thing, but what a moving sound. The impact of the sound is in what it represents, of course: the irreparable act, the ritual of the irremediable, the confrontation with absolute loss, with death.

And yet the ceremony continues; the celebration of communion begins. The value of the wafer is not in its form, the perfect circle of our tradition, but in its function, the nourishment of our beings in community. Break the bread, then, into as many pieces as possible, so that all of us can be fed, so that all of us can be a part of this sharing. So that a new, perfected circle can be formed as we all hold hands, thankful, restored, mindful of loss and suffering, prayerful for the strength to live with our fragility.

Is there a way for us to apply reverence to our losses? W. H. Auden implies as much in that marvelous verse, "Wear your tribulation like a rose." But it will take all of us, together, to learn how.

Franklin and I kept learning together until his death from hepatitis B. He was gentle and gentlemanly, radiant and kind. I am reminded of Garrison Keillor's response when asked what is the meaning of life: "What keeps our faith cheerful is the extreme persistence of gentleness and humor. Gentleness is everywhere in daily life, a sign that faith rules through ordinary things: through cooking and small talk, through storytelling, . . . music and books—all the places where the gravy soaks through and grace sinks in." Franklin Brooks was a place where grace sinks in.

In a time of grief during my brother's illness, Franklin became like a brother to me. He offered words of comfort daily, but he did more than that. On a visit to Washington, he went out of his way to meet my brother. At a professional meeting in my hometown, he made a point of visiting my mother. From him I learned that to care for our friends may mean to care also for their families.

In addition to kindness, Franklin possessed a core of great courage. He came from a state where men of courage are much admired, and he enlarged, even recast, the usual Texas definition of courage. In a speech arguing for a university policy against discrimination on the grounds of sexual orientation, he said,

> This fall some of us were privileged to hear another professor talk about the best teachers people remember and why. He led us to see that what we recognized in our teachers who inspired us was honesty. Not always brilliance. Not always an exemplary home life. But honesty in what they claimed to know and to be able to explain and to prove. . . . For my part, nowadays, I do not worry much about whether students know that I am gay. I am concerned, instead, that they feel that I am honest—that I am "straightforward" with them about myself. Nowadays no one need suffer in silence here when there is no shame. Convinced as I am that we need protection, however, from thoughtless harm here and now and for the time being, I urge that this proposal be adopted.

Franklin's generosity of spirit reminds me of that of Nikos Kazantzakis. Kazantzakis's wife, Helen, reported this conversation with her husband as he lay gravely ill in a clinic in Germany:

> "Come quickly, I have very good news," he called.
> "Very good?"
> "Yes. Very, very good."
> "The Nobel," I cried, very excited. Max Tay had received a telephone call from Stockholm, promising it to him. "The Nobel! Hurrah!"

The Nobel Prize had just been awarded not to Kazantzakis but to Albert Camus. Kazantzakis was the only person in the whole university clinic at Freiburg who failed to feel disappointed when the prize was awarded to Camus.

"Friendship is dearer to me than all the prizes in the world, Lenotschka," Nikos said to his wife. "Come quickly to help me draft a good telegram. Juan Ramon Jimenez, Albert Camus—

these are two men who well deserved the Nobel. Let's go draft a good telegram!"

Kazantzakis died a few days later. On March 16, 1959, Helen Kazantzakis received this telegram from Albert Camus:

> Madame, I was very sorry not to be able to take advantage of your invitation. I have always nurtured much admiration and, if you permit me, a sort of affection for your husband's work. I had the pleasure of being able to give public testimony of my admiration in Athens, at a period when official Greece was frowning upon her greatest writer. The welcome given my testimony by my student audience constituted the finest homage your husband's work and acts could have been granted. I also do not forget that the very day when I was regretfully receiving a distinction that Kazantzakis deserved a hundred times more, I got the most generous of telegrams from him. Later on, I discovered with consternation that this message had been drafted a few days before his death. With him, one of our last great artists vanished. I am one of those who feel and will go on feeling the void that he has left.

Kazantzakis and Camus—two good people, alike in nobility, helping each other become better.

Because reciprocity at some level is a characteristic of the classical model of mentoring, friendships of this order usually occur among people who know each other personally. Carolyn Heilbrun, however, raises another possibility. In her essay "Unmet Friends," Heilbrun speaks of how women seek out the lives of other women who have braved the same sort of fears they have chosen for themselves and whose struggles can be appropriated into their own lives. To find such friends, one must be a great reader. "Women catch courage from the women whose lives and writings they read, and women call the bearer of that courage friend." For Heilbrun, such a friend is the poet Maxine Kumin, Heilbrun's exact contemporary whom she has never met but all of whose poems and essays she reads. "Why," she asks, "do I feel, not having met her but having read all her work, that she and I are closer in the destinies we have chosen than I am to many friends personally known?"

The answer to Heilbrun's question may lie in the many ways of Athena in the *Odyssey*. At every level of her own life, Heilbrun identifies with Kumin: love of animals, a passion for writing, a long marriage, children, a high capacity for friendship, similar attitudes toward public expectations. Her friend comes to her as a sister, not through the lock of her bedroom door but through the phenomenon of the printed page, a passageway quite as mysterious and empowering.

8

POLITICS AS WORK FOR THE WORLD

Odysseus and his gallant son charged straight at the front lines,
slashing away with swords, with two-edged spears and now they
would have killed them all, cut them off from home if Athena,
daughter of storming Zeus, had not cried out in a piercing voice that
stopped all fighters cold, "Hold back, you men of Ithaca, back from
brutal war! break off—shed no more blood—make peace at once!"
. . . .
So she commanded. [Odysseus] obeyed her, glad at heart.
And Athena handed down her pacts of peace between both sides
for all the years to come—the daughter of Zeus whose shield is
storm and thunder.

Odyssey 24.579–85, 598–602

In her last appearance in the *Odyssey*, which is also the scene that concludes the epic, Athena focuses explicitly on peace for the entire community, not just for certain of its members. The survivors of the suitors killed by Odysseus and his father and son have marshalled to attack Odysseus and his household in revenge for the slaughter of their sons and brothers in the great hall of the palace. Athena definitively intervenes to stop the series of revenge murders that marks any uncivilized world where rage displaces reason. Politics, like etiquette, helps us get along together without killing each other.

I once met a young woman whose intention is to be president of the United States. A person of intelligence, confidence, and grit, she had already taken, at age twenty, remarkable steps in that direction. She just might make it. In our conversation she seemed more concerned about what her husband would be called than about how she would get elected. After consulting the etiquette books, which have not yet addressed this matter, we decided on "Mr. Jones." It is the democratic solution after all, the American way.

What my young friend does not yet know, cannot know because of her years, is that her ambition is still confined in her private world, framed by her individual gifts and aspirations. Soon she will come to understand that politics is far larger than elective office. Politics is the world of the *polis*, of the city writ large, of the social realm without which individuals cannot flourish. It is the land we all inhabit and cultivate together with others. Aristotle knew early that being part of the civil community defines us as truly human.

Politics not only orders and defines community but arises out of it. I was well into adulthood before I learned that truth. When I did, I learned it primarily from and among women— the very population Aristotle excluded, along with slaves and children, from politics and therefore from true humanity altogether.

My education began with a bill in the Tennessee legislature, came closer to home with events concerning the status of women at the university where I teach, and finally was confirmed by the example of a woman I feel I know but never met. In the course of these events I learned also the hardest lesson of all. Efforts toward a more just ordering of society almost always require confrontation. Confrontation means that some people are not going to like you. Nothing in my heart strangely warmed by Methodist good intentions prepared me for that startling outcome.

When I moved to Nashville in 1969, the university where I now teach did not hire women. I do not know if that was by policy or practice, only that a dean at the time told my parents that it was too bad I could never teach there. By the greatest of good fortunes, I was hired to direct the honors program at Fisk University, one of the oldest historically African American institutions to focus on the humanities.

Celeste Jones, a student in the honors program, had graduated from Shaker Heights High School near Cleveland and wanted to experience education in a primarily African American setting. Her poise and quiet strength transcended her years, and as we got to know each other, we began to share stories, one of which is recounted in chapter 3.

Soon we learned of House Bill 20. Introduced into the Tennessee state legislature by a representative named Larry Bates from rural west Tennessee, the legislation would have required the sterilization of women on welfare. Together Celeste and I decided to do something about it, but we did not know where to begin.

Marian Fuson, a longtime Quaker activist whose husband Nelson taught on the Fisk faculty, introduced us to JoAnn Bennett. At that time JoAnn was legislative research librarian for the Tennessee Legislative Council. She invited Celeste and me to the state capitol, where she introduced us to Molly Todd and Jane Eskind, lobbyists for the League of Women Voters. These three women taught us politics. They showed us how to look up the status of a bill in the legislature and how to identify the members of the relevant committees. More important, they told us who was important and how best to approach them.

I remember vividly our call on "Mr. Jim" Cummins, the

dean of the legislature who must have been in his eighties at the time. His eyes twinkled when we told him why we were there and what we were concerned about. "Oh," he said, "you mean the bill introduced by Master Bates? I think we can take care of that."

He did. The bill was defeated.

My friendships with these remarkable women continued. After graduation, Celeste moved to Chicago. She and colleagues began the first community health clinic run by African Americans in Chicago, but its funding was later cut by Congress. Celeste died of breast cancer in her mid-thirties. I miss her still. Jane Eskind has since run for statewide office and is a national leader in the Democratic Party. JoAnn Bennett serves as secretary of the board of directors of the Legal Aid Society of Middle Tennessee. She is a leader also in the continuing education program of her alma mater. We are in a book club together.

Then there was Molly Todd. During the civil rights movement Molly and others from Church Women United organized support for the students from Fisk and Tennessee State University who were conducting sit-ins at lunch counters in the downtown department stores. When the students were arrested, the women would sit down in their places.

While it is not uncommon in my city for well-placed women to engage in politics much more progressive than that of their husbands, the case of Molly Todd was extraordinary. Her husband, Jim Todd, was one of the highest officials in a department store with a segregated lunch counter in the 1960s. Molly did not just go along with plans for a demonstration there. She proposed it. Jim did not support her in this or most of her other activities, but he never said a word. They had an understanding. They also had a long, productive, and as far as I know, very happy marriage.

Some years later Molly and I participated in a demonstration in Oak Ridge, Tennessee, against building the Clinch River Breeder Reactor. President Carter was in town, and we made sure he saw our placards. Molly was everywhere. I remarked to her at the time that she was the first seventy-year old cheerleader I had ever seen. She threw her head back and laughed heartily.

Confronting Power
Closer to Home

I learned my next political lessons in my own backyard. I did not have to go to north Nashville or the state capitol or East Tennessee to learn them, and therefore they were much harder. Nor did they have to do with elective politics, but with the politics of prejudice and the peculiar self-righteousness of tradition. What I mean to say is, they had to do with power and institutions. This time they had to do with *me*.

Katherine Anne Porter says somewhere that it took ten years for her to understand things that happened to her. I know what she means. That many years and more have passed since the events I am about to tell, and I am still learning their impact on me. For the biggest stories, it also takes that long to be able to leave enough out to write about them.

Even so, I can more easily begin with the story of Nina, a cherished friend who serves on the same faculty and with whom I have shared tea and thoughts regularly for the past twenty-five years. Nina was born in Latvia and was twice a refugee from the politics of a war that nearly destroyed her family. Her measureless intelligence earned her a Harvard Ph.D. and a fine scholarly career, but nothing prepared her for what she would experience as the faculty cochair of the Chancellor's Commission on the Status of Women at our university. The Commission was appointed in 1975 at the request of a small group of professional women on campus, a group for which we had to cast a wide loop to gather even that many.

To this day I am not sure that anyone except us expected the Commission to amount to much.

The Commission's report after three years of study stated as its highest priority the establishment of a Women's Center, followed closely by provision of child care on campus. What became the Margaret Cuniggim Women's Center was established after further persuasion in 1978. In time, most of the other recommendations were implemented. The Commission was the first turning point for women in the university.

Before the Commission, Nina had not been politically active. Now she is, and she can name the ways the experience changed her. First, she was working with strong women and a few very supportive men. Together they empowered one another. Second, Nina was not ambitious within the system. She was an outlier, one who was marginalized but also—partly because of the feeling of marginalization—not pursuing ordinary forms of institutional advancement. Third, as she puts it, she was naive. She did not know what could not be done.

Nina may have been naive, but she also was canny. She and others in the group decided to request permission to employ a research staffer for the Commission. The young woman who was hired knew how to solicit views not only of faculty and students, but also staff. She hosted brown bag luncheons, gathering anecdotes from everyone from departmental secretaries to female student athletes. In this way the Commission not only strengthened its eventual report but also enhanced a sense of community among women on campus. Their views became important because they were heard and recorded.

Partly with the help of a law school faculty member, Nina learned how to negotiate once the report was completed. Since the report had to be approved by the university lawyers, this helped even the playing field. Specifically, Nina learned the power of silence when repeatedly challenged by the lawyers on the same sticky points in the report. When met with silence, the other side eventually had to say, "All right, let's go on to the next point." Nina also learned to conceive and articulate the larger perspective behind individual recommendations.

Finally, Nina did what any leader must do to keep at it for very long. She made sure she had a quietly supportive circle of friends behind her in this most public endeavor of her life. For Nina this included a spiritual advisor from her church, someone who shared and supported her conviction that the work she was doing was God's work, done in behalf of justice. At the same time, this kind of support helped her avoid overzealousness and grandiosity.

Nina's new abilities and hard-won confidence enabled her a little later to accept election as chair of the University Senate. Her status as a respected and admired senior faculty member continues.

Nina and I laugh about how she is always a couple of years ahead of me in life's major experiences. So it was with confronting the power structure at our university.

For me the issues were women's studies and the promotion of women to tenured ranks of the faculty. At the beginning, this all seemed fairly benign. Some students had come to me in the fall of 1971 asking for a course in women's studies. Embarrassed as I am now to confess it, I told them I was not interested. I had just come to Vanderbilt from Fisk and saw race as the only and all-compelling issue; I still believe it is the most intransigent. I admonished the students that it would take at least two years to get a new course into the curriculum. "When do you want it?" I asked. "This spring," they said. More naive than I, they got the course instituted, for the spring, as a special topics course in the philosophy department.

Soon I came to see the importance of this field of academic study and served for several years as the course coordinator. It was not an easy task. I still remember an administrator saying in 1974 that women's studies "was a fad whose time had come and gone." Nevertheless we persisted. The program began to flourish when a brilliant young English professor named Elizabeth Langland ("one of the two brightest new Ph.D.'s in English in the country—and we got her," one of her colleagues said at the time) was appointed to head the Women's Studies Committee shortly after her arrival at Vanderbilt in 1975. Among Elizabeth's research interests was the study of women in literature, and she was already publishing pioneering material in the field.

In due time Elizabeth was recommended for promotion with tenure by her department, the first woman ever in the history of that one-hundred-year-old English department. We were delighted but not surprised. She is that good. Then, after delaying the announcement until summer when students and faculty had left and all seemed quiet, the dean announced that he did not concur with the recommendation, in effect terminating Professor Langland's employment by the university at the end of the following academic year.

That, he must have thought, would be the end of that.

What the dean could not have known was the context into which he was delivering his decision that Saturday morning in mid-June, right before he left for vacation. During the previous twelve months, the university had already lost some five women from key positions. I was hired at Vanderbilt in 1971 and was tenured in 1975. Of some thirty women hired after me in the following decade in the College of Arts and Science, not one eventually gained tenure. Many left in discouragement even before their tenure decisions arrived. Faculty women had been meeting informally throughout the year to address these disturbing issues, sometimes conferring also with the two or three women members of the Board of Trust.

That Saturday morning, I went to visit Elizabeth just after

she received the news from the chair of her department. "I'm going to fight this," she told me. "Why?" I asked. "So my daughter won't have to," she replied. "All right," I told her, "I will help you—and we will do it in such a way that we will win even if we lose."

Later that morning I attended part of a conference on semiotics hosted by the university. I still do not know what semiotics is, but I was fascinated by a paper delivered by a friend of mine in classics from another institution. She discussed the passage in Plato's dialogue *Politicus* in which Socrates defines the ideal ruler as a weaver, one who weaves together the various parts of the body politic, rather than imposing power from above as a tyrant. My friend pointed out that weaving was a peculiarly feminine image for Socrates to evoke for a political function that belonged entirely to men. "Weave," I mulled to myself. "WEAV.—Women's Equity at Vanderbilt." Thus our organization came to have a name even before it existed.

The informal women's group had already scheduled a meeting for the coming Monday evening. With news of the decision about Elizabeth, we invited others to join us. That night, with clarity, determination, and certain knowledge of the enormity of what lay ahead, we decided to organize. We had agonized long enough.

What I did not know until later was that two remarkable women at the meeting, both employed in staff positions at the university, had lunch together the next day. One said to the other, "You know, these faculty women have good ideas, but they don't know anything about organizing. We'll have to teach them how to do it." And they did.

We began by identifying five means of influencing the university: publicity, pressure from alumni/ae, money, federal agencies, and the federal courts. We went after all five.

The local newspapers were intrigued that women were challenging the male hegemony of the university and, by extension, its traditional base of financial and institutional support in the surrounding community. The publicity was continuous as the case made its way through appeal procedures and finally into federal court. One Sunday morning my husband handed me the newspaper with a quotation from Susan B. Anthony, which was juxtaposed with another from Susan F. Wiltshire. Ashley's comment warmed my heart: "Susan, I'm sure there were many good reasons for you not to add my last name when we got married, but I'm proud you did."

Early one New Year's Day, Will D. Campbell telephoned me at home. "Susan," he drawled in his unreconstructed Mississippi inflection, "I've been looking around for a little trouble to get into, and I can't find any better trouble than what you women are doing over there at Vanderbilt, so I'm going to poke around and scare up some national publicity." He did what he said he would do too, and eventually an excellent article by Frye Gaillard appeared in *Progressive* magazine.

I learned from Will another important lesson that morning. Since that day I have tried never to ask, "What can I do to help?" when a friend is in the ditch. I try to do something instead.

Because official quotas limited the number of women admitted to the university until 1972, the alumnae of our institution are a remarkable lot. If they graduated before the end of the 1950s, they are likely to be even smarter, because the quota for admission then was based on a ratio of something like four-to-one. One of these, Martha Warfield, helped organize an alumnae advisory board for WEAV. These women were a joy to work with and endlessly resourceful. They hosted in WEAV's behalf some thirty "educational gatherings" in the community, and as we told the present story, we also learned from them the longer story of women at the university. Mary Jane Werthan, class of 1929, for example, says that male students who were her good friends would not speak to her or any other woman student they encountered on the campus. We also learned how effective these women are in the city they usually quietly and always expertly help run.

They aided us, as did countless others in and outside the university, with fundraising to support the coming lawsuit, as well as other endeavors for gender equity. When WEAV, by then chartered by the State of Tennessee and possessed of 501(c)3 status, sent representatives to the Metro Board of Solicitations to seek permission to raise funds, the chair seemed quite stern even though the board granted our request. After the meeting, he approached one of us privately in the hall and grinned, "I used to work at Vanderbilt. It's about time. Good luck."

We raised over sixty thousand dollars, almost all of it the hard way—by asking for it. For many of us as women, particularly Southern women, this was a new experience. I figured I had gotten the hang of it when I called on a particularly influential alumna of Vanderbilt, looked her straight in the eye, and asked her, "Will you help us raise five thousand dollars?" "I'll try," she replied without hesitation. I remember also the secretary I visited one day to tell about what we were doing. She opened her wallet and gave WEAV everything in it. "I've been waiting twenty years for this moment," she said.

We went through the procedures of filing a complaint at the Equal Employment Opportunity Commission, but by now Ronald Reagan was president and had appointed Clarence Thomas as head of the Commission. Clearly there was little interest in pursuing a sex-discrimination case. That process, however, cleared the way to federal district court.

The day the lawsuit was filed, Vanderbilt announced that it was going to establish a child care center on campus. A year later, we lost the lawsuit. That same week, the chancellor instructed the dean to appoint a director of women's studies at a tenured level, a move we had been requesting for fifteen years. Another year later, we lost the case on appeal in the

Sixth Circuit Court of Appeals in Cincinnati. Vanderbilt then started hiring women at the rank of full professor for the first time in its history.

From the tenure vote in the English department, to the dean, to the provost and chancellor, through the federal agencies, the federal district court, and finally the federal court of appeals, not a single woman was involved in deciding the fate or the scholarly merits of Elizabeth Langland. We felt like the suffragists: not one vote they had to win in Congress and then in thirty-six state legislatures to ratify the Nineteenth Amendment would be cast by a woman. We wanted to change all of this.

But if we are not changed by what we are helping to change, we are playing with blocks. I would never know what I know now without the initial anger, confrontation, and occasional betrayal—and, much more profoundly, without the sharing, community, humor, glory, empowerment, fun, risk-taking, hard work, new skills, and determination that filled a full three years. The stakes were high, the cause was right, the times required our best. It was the hardest public thing I ever did.

A year after the dean's decision, Elizabeth was gone from Vanderbilt and on to the outstanding academic career we all knew lay ahead, so WEAV was left to carry on the battle at home. We were many, including incredibly committed staff women (one of whom, a single parent, pledged a thousand dollars to WEAV) and most—but, alas, not all—of the women faculty. Most of our male colleagues on the faculty sided with the administration. "You have a good cause," they would sometimes say to me, "but this is not a good case." "I've asked around about you," said a dean from another college in the university. "I hear you are a good teacher and a leader, but you are no scholar." Said another, so I was told, "I don't know what Susan is complaining about. She's had lots of advantages here because she is a woman." An icon on the faculty said to me later, "I had thought I would never be able to speak to you again."

Such comments usually just made me mad. One hurt, however, because it was attributed to a woman on the staff whom I particularly admired. "Susan used to have such good judgment," the woman was quoted as saying. "Now she has gone off the deep end."

I called Will Campbell to ask him about the deep end business. Without missing a beat he replied: "The deep end is for grown-ups. The shallow water is where the kiddies play."

A horrible dream early in the WEAV experience dramatized for me how significantly I was being affected by extended conflict with people I worked with, usually respected, and often loved. In the dream I was in a cabin in the wilderness with a small group of friends who shared my commitments at the university. We were going about our allotted tasks, which seemed to have to do with preparing a meal. My job was to scale and clean a fish, which I placed on a cutting board on a worktable in the middle of the kitchen. Just as I made the first cuts with a long serrated knife around the fish's gills to cut off its head, it metamorphosed into a living mammal, something long and furry like a ferret. It was bleeding around its head from the cuts I had already made.

Almost immediately the creature changed shape again, this time into a beautiful infant child sitting on my lap. She was probably fifteen or eighteen months old, not yet talking but composed and well-knit. As she gazed at me closely but passively, I knew instinctively that she was mine, but not my daughter. Carrie has grey eyes and long blond hair, and this child had blue eyes and hair that was curly, short, and nearly black. She was very pretty and her nose was bleeding a little.

Then with a bolt of pain, I knew I had to finish the job I had begun. Strangely, incomprehensibly, it was as if she were giving permission for me to do what I had to do. I carried her over to the drainboard by the sink, completed the unspeakable deed by a sheer act of will, then turned sobbing against the cupboard, racked with grief but even at the moment knowing that what I was feeling was not guilt or remorse but relief.

The child was the child in myself, not the imaginative, creative child we are always to cherish and respect, but the passive, mute counterself. That she was so pretty and passively charming was the clue, for in the controversy at my university I had been learning, expensively, the limits of charm.

The dream, painful as it was, was freeing. So was the humor I learned in company with Catherine. The organizing genius behind WEAV, Catherine took me on as a parallel project, determined that, even if kicking and screaming, I would develop a sense of humor. Her own is without parallel, and slowly I learned, by watching her, that humor is the secular form of grace. Both remind us that we are not God. No amount of earnestness or good works will make things right. We can and must work for good as hard as we can, but in the end and along the way we still have to be able to laugh at ourselves.

Laughter makes for good politics too. Laughter is much harder to counter or intimidate than earnest argument. I finally realized that Catherine was right: if we did not have more fun than the other side, we would lose even if we won. One of the activities Catherine proposed for WEAV was an event called "The Vandy Run-Around." This was to be an organized jog through the campus that passed sites significant to the history of women at the university and concluded with a rally complete with kazoos. I did not even know what a kazoo was, and my natural as well as practiced reserve did not lend itself easily to a run-around. We did it, though, and it was fun and I learned the fine freedom that comes from making a fool of oneself for a good cause. Once the fool-making is out of the way, one can get on with living.

I learned that only when we take risks will we ever be criticized. The world is markedly tolerant of cowerers. When we are not afraid of criticism, then we are free to seek justice and also to be magnanimous. We are also free to have fun.

One of the hardest lessons I learned was about the nature of institutions. A sociology graduate student explained it to me. The highest priority of any institution, he said, is to maintain itself. With this new insight I had to revisit the two institutions I cherish most, the church and the university. In my naivete, I had thought that the purpose of the church was to propagate the good news and the purpose of the university was to foster learning. In Elizabeth Langland's case, my new friend proposed, the university was defending its power to make any decision it chose, or, as may have been the case here, defending decisions of subordinates even if their superiors knew they were wrong. I see the truth of this now, but I did not know it in advance, and I have had to think hard since then about how to relate to institutions.

Institutions such as churches, universities, and large businesses are necessary and good because they mean we do not have to invent everything over again every day. That frees our energies for getting on with our work. But all large institutions are weighted by their history and by a corporate culture that eclipses individuals. If we are employed by one, it is a challenge to live and work creatively in an environment over which we have no control.

I was institutionally loyal before WEAV, and I still am. I love the teaching and research and collegiality within a university, and I generally believe in the efficacy of institutions, including the church, to further the purposes of life.

Over the years I have developed small strategies for creative coexistence with my university. Irony and humor help immeasurably. I will always appreciate one colleague's comment after a particularly tedious faculty meeting: "Academics have an instinct for going straight for the capillary."

In the end, though, our identities must never be defined by any institution. In that sense we will always be partly outsiders in an ambiguous relationship with the structures of our lives. This ambiguity is healthy and proper.

For a while during and after the lawsuit at my university, I felt that I had been divorced from the institution. Eventually I realized that divorce was a wrong metaphor. One neither marries nor divorces institutions. Marriage is a lifetime contract between two consenting, equal adults. Employment is an agreement to lend certain abilities and interests for a period of time to a corporate structure. In *After Virtue*, Alasdair MacIntyre helps discern the difference between institutions and the virtues of individuals. He points out that the things we do and care about, which he calls practices, cannot survive very long if they are not sustained by institutions. Institutions, however, are concerned primarily with the acquisition and distribution of power, money, and status among competing individuals, while virtues and practices have to do with cooperation and the common good.

The fact that a relationship between individuals and institutions ought to be ambiguous does not mean that it cannot also be passionate. Values are at stake, and passion gives life. Carolyn Heilbrun asserts:

> As we age many of us who are privileged—not only academics in tenured positions, of course, but more broadly those with some assured place and pattern in their lives, with some financial security—are in danger of choosing to stay right where we are, to undertake each day's routine, and to listen to our arteries hardening. I do not believe that death should be

allowed to find us seated comfortably in our tenured positions.
. . . Instead, we should make use of our security, our seniority,
to take risks, to make noise, to be courageous, to become un-
popular.

To stand by does not mean to stand still. The troublemak-
ers are not the trouble. The trouble is the trouble. So we will
make noise, organize, keep the long view, and persist in having fun while we are doing it.

And maybe, just once in a while, we will have the satisfac-
tion I experienced shortly after the final conclusion of the
lawsuit at my institution. I overheard two colleagues arguing
about the merits of the case. Finally one turned to the other
and said: "Well, one thing is for sure. This university will
never be the same again."

Nor will I.

An Unmet Mentor

As in the case of unmet friends, perhaps one may permit
oneself one unmet mentor.

The presidential election of 1984 was a difficult time in my
state for the Democratic Party. The national ticket included
a woman for vice-president, and many local candidates had a
problem with that as well as with the probability of a landslide
reelection for President Reagan. In response a "Unity Day
Rally" at the Opryland Hotel was planned for all party candidates and loyalists.

The hundredth anniversary of the birth of Eleanor Roosevelt occurred the same week, so it was decided to include a
brief speech in her honor at the beginning of the occasion. I
was asked to give the speech.

I spent a week in the library reading about Eleanor Roosevelt. It was exhilarating to pass that much time in such good
company. I learned that this woman could dictate a hundred

letters a day, write six newspaper columns a week, give 150 lectures a year, talk with thousands of groups, and travel hundreds of thousands of miles in a lifetime—all because she understood democracy to mean the active and concerned participation of all its members for the sake of all its members.

Eleanor Roosevelt was a leader with a conscience. Throughout her life she demonstrated a capacity for change grounded in compassion for those who were victims. She did not inherit her conscience, but earned it through her willingness to be open to new experiences and needs. While still a young woman she renounced the upper-class status and prejudices into which she had been born, choosing instead to work in settlement houses and observe working conditions in garment factories in New York. Later she would say, "You must do the thing you think you cannot do."

She always preferred to see for herself, and her many visits—down into coal mines in West Virginia, with Appalachian farmers struggling to keep their land, with families hungry and homeless in the Depression—often led to new government initiatives and policies. When Jewish refugees seeking haven from Nazi persecution found a cool reception from the U.S. Department of State, Eleanor Roosevelt intervened effectively on their behalf. When the Daughters of the American Revolution refused to let Marian Anderson sing in Constitution Hall in 1939 because she was black, Eleanor Roosevelt promptly resigned her membership in that organization and arranged for Anderson to sing at the Lincoln Memorial instead. When the Americans for Democratic Action was under attack during the McCarthy era, Eleanor Roosevelt accepted its honorary chairmanship. Upon her death in 1962, Adlai Stevenson said of her: "She walked in the slums and ghettoes of the world, not on a tour of inspection, but as one who could not feel contentment when others were hungry."

Eleanor Roosevelt was not only compassionate, she was also smart. Because she was smart, she was an organizer. She knew that an instinct for reform was not enough and that in fact reformers may make poor politicians. She therefore worked tirelessly with others, especially the veterans of the suffrage struggle, to form strong political bases.

After Franklin Roosevelt was stricken with polio in 1922, she became the treasurer of the Women's Division of the state Democratic Party in New York and editor of its newspaper, traveling to as many as thirty towns on one trip to develop networks of local leaders. By 1924 she had been instrumental in organizing all but five counties of the state. With other groups she lobbied ceaselessly for equal pay legislation, child labor laws, subsidized housing, and other objectives first framed by the women reformers.

Always she was a persuaded and effective partisan. From her organizing for the state party in the 1920s to her gruelling campaign trips with John F. Kennedy in 1960, she never flagged in her commitment to elective politics as the lifeblood of a free society.

Eleanor Roosevelt was a leader with a conscience, an organizer, and a committed member of her party, but there was one thing she was not—she was not afraid. Having overcome the enormous fears of her own childhood, she learned to conquer fear so that at the age of seventy-five she could say, "I long ago reached the point where there is no living person whom I fear, and few challenges I am not willing to face."

Eleanor Roosevelt forgave the present every day for the sake of the future, and she taught us that only people who are not afraid can be full of mercy and grace and generosity.

I felt renewed by the spirit of Eleanor Roosevelt to continue to work for the world. At the same time I felt affirmed by my happiness in those days in the library, reading and mulling and placing the precise words together in the right place on the page for the right length. This, I saw, constituted my true vocation. For me, teaching and writing are not the cloistered endeavors I long had feared them to be, but politics. Politics, properly practiced, inclines always toward the good of the community. It is the gift we return to the *polis* that made us who we are.

9

INSTRUMENTAL
MENTORING

A thena's versatility in becoming helpful companions brings new complexity to our understanding of the term *mentor*. Athena serves as a symbol or metaphor for an imaginative world, first surfacing in Homer's *Odyssey*, that enables us to see how many people inform and enrich our lives. In the *Odyssey* Athena constantly works for the good of those about whom she cares. One thing she never does, however, is train the young to succeed in business or to become like her. She does not raise up the next generation of stars in a hierarchy over which she presides. Since she is always disguised as someone else, she can hardly be grooming people who look like her or somehow remind her of herself.

In our time, mentoring is most commonly associated with the teaching of skills for a particular task, enabling those taught to move up in some line of work, or even engendering in them self-esteem. The aim of the present chapter is to assess this mode of instrumental mentoring and to suggest some of its potential hazards. Arguments for such arrangements are many and compelling. Possible perils include conformity and exclusivity by race or class, the awkwardness of mismatches, and the abuse of authority, including the potential for sexual exploitation.

In a presidential address to a medical association, published subsequently in a professional journal, Jeremiah Barondess outlines the instrumental or professional mentoring relationship as follows:

> The mentor, ordinarily several years older, with greater experience and seniority in the world the protégé is entering, serves variously as teacher, sponsor, advisor and model: as teacher in enhancing the younger individual's skills and intellectual development; as sponsor in using his or her influence to facilitate the protégé's entry and early advancement in the field they both inhabit; as host and guide, in helping to initiate the younger person into a new occupational and social world, acquainting him or her with its values, customs, resources, and cast of characters; as advisor, providing counsel, moral support and direction; and through his or her own virtues, achievements and lifestyle, serving as an exemplar whom the protégé can seek to emulate.

Of the fifty-three entries under "mentor" in my university's library, fully half have to do, understandably, with some form of education in schools, universities, or the community. Examples include *The Role of Mentors in the Lives of Psychology Graduate Students; Mentors in Schools: Developing the Profession of Teaching; Teachers and Mentors: Profiles of Distinguished Twentieth-Century Professors of Education; Mentorship in Nursing; The Mentor's Manual: A Guide for Leaders in Boys' Work.* At least one school of education offers a course on mentoring.

Other studies outline the importance of mentors in such areas as the arts, politics, volunteer community service, and working with children, especially those at special risk.

In more recent years, increasing attention has been given

to the importance of mentors for women in the workplace and in their lives. Of the following titles, only the first was published before 1994: *The Corporate Connection: Why Executive Women Need Mentors to Reach the Top* (1982); *The Gender Bias Prevention Book: Helping Girls and Women to Have Satisfying Lives and Careers; Gender, Identity, and Self-Esteem: A New Look at Adult Development; How Women Executives Succeed; Women: A Feminist Perspective; Strangers in the Senate: Politics and the New Revolution of Women in America.*

In 1983, the Project on the Status and Education of Women of the Association of American Colleges published a paper titled "Academic Mentoring for Women Students and Faculty: A New Look at an Old Way to Get Ahead." The paper includes discussion of such topics as "How to Get Mentors to Choose You" and "Tips on How to Be a Mentor." In the conclusion, the authors point out the limits and potential of their proposals:

> Certainly mentoring is not a panacea for every academic and career problem. However, few would deny that newcomers to academe can gain much from mentoring relationships. Although in the past mentoring in academe has often served to keep the real newcomers—such as women and minorities—outside the "inner circle," individual women and men, institutions and organizations can take many steps to make mentoring available to women, and to provide newer mentoring alternatives.

There now exists a corporation devoted to helping women get ahead in business. It is, according to its literature, "a full-service firm offering a complete range of mentoring products (formal, informal, group-centered, and one-to-one) and consulting services." It operates a "comprehensive executive development program for high-potential professional women." Its signature program pairs mid-level professional women with top-level women executives from a different company. This "mentor-mentee" relationship is designed to "level the play-ing field for high-potential women" (defined as designated among the top fifteen percent in their companies) so that they may win additional promotions. The mentors in the program are required to have a "credible corporate track record" and other admirable qualities. In 1998 the cost to sign up for a mentor was $2,475.

All of these activities are potentially valuable and important. All may contribute significantly to the success of individuals. The need for such programs has grown as contemporary soci-ety has become more mobile. This mobility, as well as the in-creasingly corporate culture of society that now extends even to universities and churches, separates us from established com-munities of attentive elders.

Institutionalized mentoring, however, has drawn critics. John Siegfried, an economics professor, addresses the issue in this way:

> I despise fads of any sort, and I think mentoring is a fad. Some-times, however, perceived fads are the beginning of a sensible long-term change. . . . I am opposed to formal mentoring pro-grams. It is best done informally at lunch or something. You want to be wary about forcing your advice on people. But to sit back and let them sink or swim is undesirable too.

The risk of conformity accompanies formalized mentoring relationships. Meredith Price, an undergraduate student who finally terminated her relationship with a social sorority, de-scribes that danger in its most obvious form:

> Once we arrived in the house, I, like all the other girls, was given a mentor. This custom of giving the freshman girls an older sister in the house was bizarre to me. I was supposed to feel some secret bond with this complete stranger. She was somehow considered a sister and should have made me feel at ease. Instead I felt suffocated. . . . I did not consider myself

better because I was chosen, but I considered myself part of a
political system of exclusive conformists.

The rush to conformity does not end with adolescence and
young adulthood. One of the most callous misappropriations of
the concept of mentoring I have seen appeared on the style
pages of the *New York Times* in 1981. Anne P. Hyde, head of an
executive search firm specializing in the recruitment of women,
suggested that women on the way up should avoid associating
with "unsuccessful turkeys," even if they were their friends.
She insisted further, "Leaving your friends behind isn't disloy-
alty. You are going to be judged by the company you keep. Seek
out the people who can help you. Men have known this for
years, and we are playing in their arena." If this is the proce-
dure required for success in the world, I propose that all of us,
men and women alike, pack up and go home.

When I was in graduate school, I began to notice that certain young men in our cohort were singled out as protégés by
some of our professors. Some of the women students, I among
them, were envious. Much later I recognized the negative out-
comes that could result from such relationships. Ideally they
would come to an end at the time appropriate for the protégé.
If these pairings did not end at an appropriate time, however,
only two results were left: either the protégé would become
obsessed with surpassing or replacing his elder, or, worse, he
would eventually despair of achieving comparable status at
all. In either case, he would never be free to identify and develop his own unique capabilities.

Another danger of formalized mentoring, less obvious at
first, is that it may not encourage innovation. For a young
person wishing to try new teaching methods, for example, or
new ways of doing business, a senior mentor might discour-
age any deviations from the proven formula for success,
namely, his own.

Sometimes arranged mentor relationships can be painfully

awkward. I am still embarrassed about such situations in my own experience. In the early days of women on my university faculty, for example, we tried to match newcomers with more senior women. I felt stilted and presumptuous in this relationship. So did my young colleague. Soon, by mutual benign neglect, we let the arrangement die. In fact, I am embarrassed when I am asked to "mentor" anyone. My guess is making that role official in most cases does not work well over time. It takes too little account of the uniqueness of each individual. Besides, we are all on the journey. Even the older ones are still seeking and growing themselves. For them, at least, mentoring may be something more like this:

> Mentor
> You will not know
> the moment when
> instead of seeking
> you are sought.
>
> And if you are,
> you will not notice
> because you yourself
> will still be seeking,
> seeing and sometimes
> choosing the brambled
> byways where lie
> an abandoned cistern,
> cenotaph to souls
> that once danced close by,
> or a strange new friend,
> or a poem that will
> not let you go.
>
> Maybe, once or more,
> as you lean into a curve,
> you will catch behind you
> at the periphery of your vision

a younger one watching you,
what it is you are looking for.

A third risk in formalized or instrumental relationships can happen in any relationship: the abuse of authority. The usual definition of authority has to do with the power to determine and enforce final decisions. This sort of authority is crucial for our lives. Authority exercised from above is a true gift *when* it is exercised for the sake of the subordinate. I would never want my affection for the oblique, self-limited authority of mentors to suggest that I reject all power exercised from above. I have witnessed enough abuse of hierarchical power, however, that I was profoundly grateful for a new understanding of authority that came about at a critical moment in my life.

During the events at my university that I described in chapter 8, my friend Elizabeth Langland and I went for a leisurely run the evening before her gender-discrimination lawsuit was to be heard in federal court. We talked about various matters—my fond memory is that we also exchanged recipes. We must also have been talking about the misuse of power because Elizabeth said to me, "You know, we must never assume positions of authority until we have gained genuine authority ourselves. For me, that authority will come through reading and writing about literature."

"Yes," I knew instantly, "that's it." I remembered then that *authority* is derived from *auctus*, a form of the Latin verb *augeo*, which has to do with increase, enlargement, or new emphasis. It has little sense of hierarchy. In that moment I understood for the first time that when we "author," we begin to speak in our own voice.

Authority in this sense is spacious, not restrictive. It is hospitable, not hostile, to different voices and ideas. It is always nurturing because it enlarges the range of possibilities both for ourselves and for others. This is the authority of mentors.

The question persists of whether individuals with constituted authority over others can be their mentors at the same time. One view might hold that a mentoring relationship is compromised inescapably because the responsibility of assigning a grade or a salary or a promotion rests with one party and not the other. I formerly held that view. I now think that such relationships are possible, always informally and almost as a by-product, under two conditions.

The first condition has to do with the mentors. If those individuals choose to limit their power, take care not to exploit others, and refrain from needing the success of the younger ones to bolster their own egos, then they are true teachers whom others may choose to think of as mentors.

One example of such a teacher is a colleague in another department whom I will call William. William works with his graduate students not only to help them teach and write a dissertation, but also to choose the universities to which they will apply for jobs. He shapes the recommendations he writes for them to feature their strengths. He coauthors papers with them and works with them to bring the papers to a level acceptable to the better journals. He and his students then go their separate ways. He is not their mentor-for-life, although they may remain friends. William enjoys this process. Surely his students are grateful for it.

This leads to the second condition: It is always the younger ones who determine who their mentors are. The younger ones identify those who offer something they need, because it is they who sense most truly what is their need. That is why formally assigned mentor pairs may often fall short or fail altogether. Remember that Telemachus took the initiative of rising to greet Athena disguised as Mentes, the Taphian ship captain, at the beginning of the *Odyssey*. Athena did not approach him and announce that she had come to be his mentor.

Richard Sennett offers a nuanced discussion of the

relationship between authority and nurturance. He first dissects the error that results from confusing patriarchy with paternalism. The former is a society in which all people are consciously related by blood ties. In such a society egoism and altruism are joined, and a father may and often does sacrifice for the sake of his children.

Paternalism, largely a product of nineteenth-century industrialization, dissociated family from the means of production and substituted, as Sennett put it, "male domination without a contract." Then the captains of industry pretended to function as fathers but offered only a false love to their subjects, false because they adopted the metaphor of the benign father but had only their own interests at heart.

The notion that power should be related to nurturance, a bond long supported by traditional religion, breaks down even further in modern society, according to Sennett. Instead of the paternalism that falsely claims to be acting out of fatherly concerns, the new form of authority, exercised by autonomous figures, expresses no concern for the well-being of others at all.

Perhaps what we all yearn for, in our times of loneliness and need, is the experience of Dante at the beginning of the *Divine Comedy*. Dante is wandering in a dark wood and a dark night of the soul when the poet Vergil appears before him. Vergil, who is hoarse presumably because he has not spoken for roughly thirteen hundred years, says to Dante, "Therefore, for your own good, I think it well / you follow me, and I will be your guide / and lead you forth through an eternal place" (1.105–109). Dante is worried that he is not worthy. "Poet, you must guide, / before you trust me to that arduous passage, / look to me and look through me—can I be worthy?" (2.10–12). He insists that he is not Aeneas or St. Paul—they were worthy, but he is not.

Like Mentor to Telemachus or Odysseus, Vergil confronts Dante about his cowardice: "I understand from your words and the look in your eyes . . . your soul is sunken in that cowardice / that bears down many men, turning their course and resolution by imagined perils, as his own shadow turns the frightened horse." Then after a long account of his purposes, Vergil asks, "And now what ails you? Why do you lag? Why this heartsick hesitation and pale fright?" (2.4ff.). Dante responds to this firmness with new heart: "Just so my wilted spirits rose again, and such a heat of zeal surged through my veins that I was born anew. . . . My Guide? My Lord? My Master! Now lead on: one will shall serve the two of us in this" (end Canto 2.).

Rollo May notes in this exchange that Vergil is firm throughout, never sentimental. Yet the initiative *must* come from the one who is in need. As Dante and Vergil begin their journey toward the inferno at the end of Canto 2, it is Dante who takes the lead. Vergil was the right person in the right place to meet Dante's need, but it was the younger man who made the decision to sign up with the elder for the journey. He assumed his own authority, his own voice.

Before leaving this list of perils, I cannot fail to mention the potential for sexual exploitation in any close relationship. Plato was right that eros is central to learning and growth. That, of course, is one reason why a heterosexual mentor relationship can be problematic. A famous professor had a circle of young women protégés in his field, whom he cultivated as lovers as well as scholars. In three cases, one by one, his protégés also became his wives. The same potential for exploitation inheres, of course, with pairs of the same sex.

Having outlined its potential hazards, I affirm again the usefulness and objectives of many forms of instrumental mentoring. It is time now, nevertheless, to turn our attention to the conditions that foster mentoring in its classical form.

10

COMMUNITIES
AS MENTORS

A mentor relationship is never an end in itself. Always its purpose is to prepare the younger one to move with confidence and freedom into the world of the larger community. Mentoring is prologue toward this end. Its fruit is an individual's creative, productive life together with others in society. The reverse of this equation, however, raises the question of whether communities might themselves serve on occasion as mentors to individuals.

A biblical precedent for this possibility occurs in Numbers 11. After leading his recalcitrant people out of Egypt, Moses now must listen to their protests over the lack of meat to eat. He complains to God that he did not give birth to these people, that he is not their wet nurse, and that they are too heavy for him to carry alone. If God is going to treat him this way, he continues, he begs to be put to death right now. Moses is so angry he would rather be dead than continue.

God appears in no disguise here, although elsewhere in the

Hebrew Bible we hear of mysterious angels and messengers and voices from burning bushes. Here God speaks to Moses directly:

> Gather for me seventy of the elders of Israel, whom you know to be the elders of the people and officers over them; bring them to the tent of meeting, and have them take their place there with you. I will come down and talk with you there; and I will take some of the spirit that is on you and put it on them; and they shall bear the burden of the people along with you so that you will not bear it all by yourself. (vv. 16–17)

Here the message is to collect a community, a council of lateral mentors as it were, to share the burden and help point the way. Discernment as well as shared responsibility will result from such a gathering. The spirit and wisdom that is within Moses will be engendered among the others as well.

A wise woman once said, "Never complain alone." That advice is a sound organizing principle. Individual voices of dissent can always be easily dismissed. It is also sound advice for living. The social principle saves us from the terrifying isolation—and the sheer exhaustion—of the individual principle.

Where I come from the individual principle is captured in the phrase "pulling yourself up by your bootstraps." The metaphor does not bear close scrutiny, for gravity argues heavily against the possibility of lifting oneself very high by one's bootstraps or anything else. The creed behind the cliché, however, is familiar enough: "I can take care of this myself. Furthermore, I *will* take care of this myself." As with most truisms, this one is true most of the time. Our concern here has to do with the rest of the time.

Lutheran minister Edmund Schleicher writes of the "bootstrap syndrome" as follows:

Each of us encounters situations in life when our own efforts, no matter how vigorous or strenuous, continue to fall short of reaching a desired goal.

This applies to many physical tasks, but more especially to matters spiritual and emotional. A wealthy young man in a rather well-known Bible story had to come to a realization that, despite all his efforts, something essential still was missing. Tugging at his own bootstraps was futile, and would forever remain so.

So it is, for instance, when we are beset with what has come to be called clinical depression. No amount of resolution, no persistent determination, no amount of fervent praying even—due to erroneous expectations—will set body and mind free. At least not permanently.

The secret of freedom and deliverance is to acknowledge that all this pulling at one's own bootstraps won't do the job. Having said and done and thought all we could, we eventually must reach a moment when we are ready to sit back, relax, and let someone or something other than self take hold of our psychological and emotional bootstraps—not merely to assist us in pulling them on, but to pull them and us out from the morass we are in to the higher ground where we want and need to be.

The capacity to give ourselves over to the wisdom of others is fitting not only in crisis situations but also in other significant occasions of a life journey.

Because of the absence in our family's Protestant tradition of occasions to mark a child's transition into young adulthood, my husband and I arranged for a version of a bar or bat mitzvah for our son and daughter as each turned thirteen. Each child invited twelve special adult friends to come on a Sunday afternoon to gather around the dining room table. These friends brought words of advice, caution, humor, or exhortation to share. Later we gathered the written version of their remarks into scrapbooks for the children to keep for the future.

On these two occasions I sensed that our community of friends was gathering not only around the well-being of our children but around itself as well. When we give of our best to others, we give gifts also to ourselves.

Recently I have heard of two occasions on which couples nearing retirement have invited a community of friends for a retreat to help them decide what to do next, or, as one of them says, "what we should do when we grow up."

These are examples of the benevolent community, perhaps more generous and less problematic because of their ad hoc, provisional status. It is possible, of course, that members of close associations might enforce conformity on one another in ways that diminish rather than cultivate life, just as individual mentors might foster conformity. This sort of thing happens, paradoxically, even in churches. My experience of both communities and individuals, however, has been that the more secure they are, the more hospitable they are to difference.

I think of how comforted Moses must have been to see those seventy elders gathered around him. God could have told him just to buck up, raise his chin, quit complaining, and move on. Instead, God put companions at his side to share the journey with him. Such companions as these become our mentors, even if they appear first as strangers.

11

HOSPITALITY
TO STRANGERS

odern hospitality is a transaction among friends—for example, an invitation to close acquaintances to come for dinner or a party. Ancient hospitality, on the other hand, was a transaction among strangers. One's survival, not merely one's happiness, often depended on it. In antiquity the relationship between host and stranger was so charged and precarious that the gods—Zeus in the Greek world and Yahweh in the Hebrew—take care to protect it. The Talmud boldly asserts that hospitality to strangers is greater than welcoming the presence of God.

One day I drove from our farm to a small town nearby to locate a welder to help with some minor repairs. When I telephoned the gentleman whose name I had been given, his wife told me that he was out but would be home soon. I stopped by later, knocking tentatively at the back door because it was lunchtime. His wife answered and invited me to come in and join them for lunch.

I was in the process of declining, saying I would come back later, when the welder himself appeared, napkin still in hand. He also urged me to come in for lunch and described the food on the table. My real hunger overcame my theoretical inhibitions, and I accepted.

Many plates were passed, good stories were shared, and dessert was served before my hosts asked my name, my purpose for coming, or the most important question in that culture, who my people were.

What I was offered that day was an act of hospitality in the ancient sense rather than the modern. Hospitality to strangers, weighted as it is with strict and sometimes fearful obligations, takes on new meaning and new urgency in a modern world in which we are surrounded by so many people we do not know.

People who live in cities are surrounded by strangers. While I do not know personally a single Ethiopian, Pakistani, or Finn, I also do not know many of the people who live in my own neighborhood or even city block. I have read that no one in the United States is more than six people away from knowing anyone else, but that abstraction does not change the fact that most of the people around us are strangers.

A tea party hosted by my mother when I was eleven changed my life. We invited only two guests: Mrs. Ivey, the principal of the nearby elementary school my brothers and I all attended, and Mrs. Simmons, the principal of the elementary school for African American children miles across town. My mother had met Mrs. Simmons through one of her volunteer activities, liked her, and thought the two principals would enjoy knowing one another.

I always loved school (except for the fifth grade, when I had a teacher who clearly preferred boys to girls) and looked forward to this occasion. With the peculiar innocence of children who have to learn the prejudices of their society, I did not know what racism was until I saw it. As we sat drinking our tea in front of the fireplace, my mother, Mrs. Simmons, and I were chatting and having a wonderful time. After a while I began to notice, however, how Mrs. Ivey sat in near silence, patently agitated at being in this mixed company. My innocence ended that day.

It is also true that the people we know best—spouses, lovers, roommates, friends—are all in some sense strangers. If we have children, they are strangers too. There are things about them we will never know. (In the case of teenagers, there are things we *hope* we will never know.) Our parents, whether they are living or not, are also strangers. We are able to know them even less well than our children, and we will keep discovering things about them long after they are dead.

I have never written much about my father, partly because my relationship with him was so complex. I look like him. I loved some of his qualities but had a hard time respecting him—he wore his flaws of temperament and need on his sleeve. I toughened through my conflicts with him, which is probably why I have never been sufficiently deferential to constituted authority. In our respective ways, we were devoted to one another. These days I realize I hardly knew him, so I delight in learning more, even twenty years after his death, as I did in the matter of the iris.

Planting Iris

I loved iris for years before I planted any,
then a hundred over a week or more
one fall when I was over fifty.

As I dug I puzzled where I got it from,
why I wanted to plant iris more than
any other thing I might have done,

could think of no one in my family
who cared much for flowers anyway
except for one great-grandmother
who died the day that I turned five.

When the work was done I called my mother,
told her of the planting, she said
Oh Susan not a spring went by
that your father did not say he wished
he had planted iris the fall before.

So then I knew, one tiny piece I had
not known, never heard him say it,
but knew it true in the marrow of my bone.

Bone? Is the love of iris buried deep
there too in some unfathomable cotillion
of spiraling gyres of DNA?

If I could know only one lettered
sequence of the four nucleotides
of one gene of one chromosome
of those twenty-three resolute pairs
that cast me upon the shore
as who I thought I only was,

what more might I yet learn
of the abyss that is the parent
I deigned to think I knew
but did not know loved iris?

The stranger is also our own selves. Julia Kristeva questions the ideas and institutions of the "foreigner" or "stranger" in various cultures including ancient Greece. She holds that we all have strangeness or the stranger within our psyche, which is finally the source of the "stranger."

The more we realize our own strangeness, the more open we become to other strangers, including the stranger who may be a god. When we are bursting with self-assurance and certitude, when we know ourselves absolutely and are confident that we are right, there is little propensity for openness to other possibilities.

Real differences separate us in this patchwork world of ours. Our chances for transcending those differences are increased when we welcome strangers with an act of hospitality that does not rely on familiarity or affection or approval. Political as well as personal life depends on the openness that permits us to deal creatively with others not like ourselves. Hospitality to strangers transforms outsiders into friends and may also transform us.

A story from Luke 24 shares at least one feature with the *Odyssey:* the tendency of divine visitors to disappear as soon as they are recognized. Two of Jesus' followers are walking along on the road to Emmaus, a village about seven miles from Jerusalem, shortly after Jesus' crucifixion. A stranger appears to them and asks what they are talking about. They reply, "Are you the only stranger in Jerusalem who does not know the things that have taken place there in these days?" "What things?" he asks. "The things about Jesus of Nazareth," they answer.

The stranger himself then begins to tell the story and interpret the events according to scripture. Incredulous, they beg him to remain with them. When they reach Emmaus, they sit down for a meal together. At the table, the stranger blesses the bread, breaks it, and gives it to them. Luke writes that at this moment "their eyes were opened, and they recognized him; and he vanished from their sight." Sometimes companion mentors, even when they are deities, do not stay around very long.

Being open to strangers or to the strangeness within ourselves is perilous business. Parker Palmer speaks of these dangers: "Openness to the stranger, and to letting the stranger be, is resisted by the basic dynamics of community formation. . . .

The stranger threatens the foundations of such a community by blurring the boundary; the stranger must either be kept out or made to become like us." Openness to the new, however, is critical for change, which is the purpose of mentoring.

Philip Roth writes of these perils in his extraordinary short story, "The Conversion of the Jews." In Roth's story, Oscar Friedman at the age of thirteen is going through his bar mitz-vah classes with Rabbi Bender. Oscar has the unfortunate habit of asking unexpected questions. When he gets conven-tional answers, he says to the rabbi, "But I meant something different." The rabbi is not amused, and when this happens once too often, he calls Oscar's mother to have her ask her son what the problem is at the bar mitzvah class. Oscar tells her, "I asked the question about God, how, if He could create the heaven and earth in six days and make all the animals and the fish and the light in six days—the light especially, that's what always gets me—that He can make the light. Anyway, I asked Rabbi Bender if He could make all that in six days, and if God could pick the six days he wanted right out of nowhere, why couldn't he let a woman have a baby without having inter-course." Oscar's mother slaps him when she hears the ques-tion, just as Rabbi Bender had done.

The conflict escalates until finally Oscar runs to the top of the synagogue and threatens to jump. A crowd gathers below on the street, begging him not to. Finally Oscar shouts down to his mother and the rabbi: "Promise me, promise me you'll never hit anybody about God. You should never hit anybody about God."

Oscar Friedman was worried not so much about the virgin birth as about our hitting people in the name of God. He knew that when we hit people because we think we know all about God, we do not know God. Oscar was arguing for hospitality toward the stranger who is God and toward all the strangers who are God's people.

The ancient Greeks as well as Jews and Christians believed that the stranger at our door or at our side might be a divinity. Divinities come in disguise, however, because their manifest presence would be more than mortals could bear. By being open to strangers, we may sometimes have the glimmering sense, over our shoulder and just out of reach, that we have been in the presence of something transcending ourselves.

That is how Telemachus felt after his first encounter with Athena in the form of the visiting ship captain, Mentes. Homer tells us that this meeting, for a moment at least, made Telemachus feel godlike himself:

Off and away Athena the bright-eyed goddess flew like a bird in soaring flight but left his spirit filled with nerve and courage, charged with his father's memory more than ever now. He felt his senses quicken, overwhelmed with wonder—this was a god, he knew it well and made at once for the suitors, a man like a god himself.

Odyssey 1.367–73

12

TIME TO BE AVAILABLE

A painful experience taught me a new perspective about time. On a family visit to Washington I was hurrying across the cavernous National Air and Space Museum with my three-year-old daughter by the hand. We were supposed to meet the rest of our family at a certain hour, and I was determined to be there on time. Our daughter was distressed but doing the best she could, taking two or three steps to my one.

Then in a flash, I realized it: For me to accomplish all the things I thought I had to do required speed and concentration, the very parental qualities most antithetical to the needs of a child. Now I know there is no such thing as "quality time," just time proper, for us to do with as we choose.

In *The Workaholics*, Wayne Oates has written the classic exposé of the perversion that results from equating one's work with one's worth. Work becomes all-consuming when we buy into the belief that success, achievement, and even mere activity are virtuous, and that failure or lack of achievement or inactivity are sinful or useless. Oates identifies the symptoms of a work addict as follows: (1) an insistence on going to work early or staying late or both, frequently coupled with the need to talk about how much we are working, (2) comparing how much work we are able to get done with that of someone else, (3) an inability to say no to people who want our services or our time, assuming that no one else can do the job as well as we, and (4) relegating emotional responsibilities not related to our job to other people so that the one all-consuming need for work can be pursued without complications.

In one of his classes Oates asked his students to describe the qualities of their parents. Those with work-addicted parents used words like preoccupation, haste, irritability, and depression. Oates suggests that modern popular religion has made the traits of a workaholic a sort of religious, though not a Christian, virtue and that workaholism needs to be reexamined under the scrutiny of unalloyed Christianity. Reform for workaholics, according to Oates, occurs by means of a rich inner life of contemplation, through which we filter what is and what is not truly important for our lives.

Douglas Steere writes in *Work and Contemplation* of occasional moments of transcendence, as "ripples of ecstasy, when our deepest creative impulse, our spring of freedom, is drawn upon and released. . . . And in such moments of utter self-absorption, we are lifted above both pain and pleasure." These moments move us beyond the ordinary labors of our lives. They often occur when we have been in the company of strangers. They require time, and they invite love.

Rachel Maddux once said to a group of young writers, "I have heard aspiring writers complain that they couldn't 'write dialogue,' that it didn't sound real. That's not where the trouble is. The thing that's wrong is that they haven't heard it, and, behind that, the thing wrong is that they did not love the people to whom they were listening, one at a time." It takes time to listen, at least to listen to one person as if at that moment there were no one else in the world.

Rachel told the writers also about a cook who baked wonderful cakes. When on the rare occasion one fell, she would say, "Everything is in there that should be, but I just left the love out of that one; I was in a hurry."

The lack of hurry is the most striking feature of the central story of the *Bhagavad Gita*, the most important and influential religious text of India and the Hindu story known best in the West.

Many years ago, a stranger came to me in person of P. Lal, a scholar, poet, translator, and publisher of Indian literature in English from Calcutta. As a visiting professor at the University of Illinois, Lal gave a guest lecture in my humanities course that startled me out of my conventional modes of thinking and started a long journey of connections that continues still.

It was Professor Lal who first told me about the *Bhagavad Gita*. He gave me a copy of his own translation, which he calls a "transcreation," of the great Indian epic. Decades later, when I told a close friend I was writing about mentors, I saw her turn to her daughter and whisper, "Krishna and Arjuna." There was the *Bhagavad Gita* again, just when I needed it.

Arjuna is poised for battle on the plain of Kuru when he looks across the field and sees his kinsmen, teachers, and friends. He is horrified at the thought of waging war against people he knows and loves, and he determines he cannot fight. To his charioteer, who is Lord Krishna in disguise, he says, "We don't know which weight is worse to bear—our conquering them or their conquering us."

Krishna engages in dialogue with Arjuna about how one is to live, centered always on detachment and sacrifice. "Action imprisons the word unless it is done as sacrifice; freed from attachment, Arjuna, perform action as sacrifice!" Krishna continues, "Always perform with detachment any action you must do; performing action with detachment, one achieves supreme good." In the course of this long conversation, Arjuna recovers his spirit: "Seeing your gentle human form, Krishna, I recover my own nature, and my reason is restored."

Though the text of Krishna's counsel is brief, the entire conversation if read aloud would take longer than two hours. Professor Lal told me that the *Bhagavad Gita* was the book that most inspired Thoreau at Walden. Later I learned that among Gandhi's handful of possessions at his death was a well-thumbed copy of Thoreau's *Civil Disobedience*. Still later, I came to know the impact of Gandhi's life and work on Martin Luther King Jr., as well as on Dietrich Bonhoeffer and many other resisters to violence and injustice. Pete Seeger says that school children in India are being taught to sing these days, in their own languages and dialects, "We Shall Overcome." And the Rev. Mel White has traveled in India to study soul force as a way of countering homophobia in this country.

This story makes its wonderful repeating loops through place and time: from a conversation on the battlefield at Kuru between Arjuna and the god Krishna, to a pond in Massachusetts, to Gandhi's ashrams in India, to Montgomery, Alabama, to school children in India, and now back to the United States in the struggle for acceptance of gays and lesbians—all because a transcendent presence took all the time necessary to talk about how to live a life with a young prince on his way into battle.

To discern such presences or fully to be present to others takes time. I once heard a story about a seminary class in which students studying the parable of the Good Samaritan were given three different sets of instructions. In each case, however, they were to report to another building on the campus. The first group was allowed very little time to reach the second site. The second group was given a little more time. The third group had no time limit at all. From our own experiences it is easy to envision which group stopped to help an "injured" student near the sidewalk on the way to the second building.

At a funeral service at a Missionary Baptist Church I sang a hymn I had never heard before, "I'm Available to You." It is a new gospel song, written by Carlis Moody, Jr., and recorded by the Rev. Milton Brunson and the Thompson Community Singers. The message centers on having time to be available:

> I have emptied out my cup, so that you can fill me up.
> Now I'm free, I just want to be more available to you.
> . . . .
> Use me Lord to show someone the way
> And enable me to say
> My storage is empty
> And I am available to you.

Above the door in my office hangs a poster of a stylized tree with a few red fruits like apples. My poster has no text, but I once saw one otherwise identical to it that included a quotation from the Indian poet Tagore: "The shade of my tree is for passersby. Its fruit, for those for whom I wait." The poster serves as a reminder that my shade is available for every student I teach. Such fruit as I may have to offer will go to I know not whom. I simply wait, that's all. Maybe, sometime, at times of their own choosing, some of those for whom I wait will appear at my door. If they do, I hope I will be available, for I know they will bring gifts in their coming.

Lewis Hyde speaks of the reciprocity that inheres in the exchange of gifts not of commerce but of the spirit he calls eros. Under the aegis of such gifts, we possess the ability to grow into new life. Hyde adds that it is up to us to develop the gifts we receive, and in that completion is our gratitude. The final act of gratitude, however, is to pass the gift on to others.

It takes time both to give and to receive gifts that matter. This kind of time cannot be scheduled or slotted into a daily reminder book. It is accidental time, something different from chronological time. The only way we can know its gift is to wait, to be open, to be available, both to ourselves and to others.

13

THE JOURNEY
CONTINUES

The goddess still kept Mentor's build and voice.

Odyssey 24.602

In her last appearance in the *Odyssey*, the scene that ends the epic, Athena once again assumes the form of Mentor. The quotation above is a translation of the last line of the Greek text, of which the final word is "Mentor." To the very end, the divine Athena maintains the disguise of an everyday friend, a person fully incorporated in the familiar community.

Throughout the *Odyssey*, Athena pulls alongside those whose need makes them open to help. She offers the right words in the right place at the right time, thereby empowering her companions to do for themselves whatever it is they uniquely must do. She helps people become themselves.

Athena combines the characteristics of tour guide, symphony conductor, family therapist, senior policy advisor, and delightful companion with a sense of humor. The journeys of Odysseus, Telemachus, and Penelope are our journeys too.

Jenny Strauss Clay speaks for many readers of this epic "with
all its charm, toughness, and wisdom":

> For those who study the Odyssey over a long period of time, this
> poem becomes their book. We each live it in our own fashion;
> to study the poem of Return means to make our own return.
> Those who are bold enough to write on the Odyssey experience
> in turn the terrors and temptations of a marvelous journey.

Our journey in these pages has been to explore the ways
mentoring occurs in the Odyssey and in our lives. The classical model of mentors derives from the various identities assumed by Athena in her role as helpful companion to the
main characters in the Odyssey. In these disguises Athena im-
parts to each individual the courage and insight required to
become one's best self. She empowers others for the sake of
their own life journeys. In the contemporary instrumental
model, on the other hand, a mentor typically is seen as a
person ahead of us, usually a superior in our profession, who
serves as a role model and sponsor for our success up the
ladder.

Our human lives are richer and more various than any ex-
ternal achievement the world can bestow. In the classical
model elaborated here, mentors have our interest rather than
their own at heart. They never want us to become like themselves. Rather, they care about us enough to want us to become
who we are, discerning and living out the gifts that are uniquely
our own, both individually and within our communities.

Mentors may be attentive elders we know very well. Certain family members may be the best mentors of all. Sometimes the helpful stranger may be a child, an artist, or a mere
bystander whom we never see again. Almost always we will
find mentors among our friends.

In living with such companions at our side, we seek far
more than merely individual goal-fulfillment. True mentors
stand with us in our work for the world, for they know that the

well-being of the community is crucial for the well-being of all its members.

The classical model of mentors requires a rethinking of gender. In those places where constituted power still resides mostly in men, achievement for women and other outsiders will necessarily require the support of male supporters. Thank goodness for the good men who provide such support, otherwise the structures could never be changed.

Identifying women as mentors in our lives opens us also to guidance from everyone else, including the powerless. Children or passersby do not have the status of any constituted power, but in mysterious ways they sometimes offer transformative gifts. My grandfather liked to advise, "Don't hang around poor people. They can't do you any good." The question I should have asked him, of course, was, "What kind of good do you have in mind?"

In one of her mystery novels, Carolyn Heilbrun dissects the matter of maternal comfort in a dialogue between two female academics:

> "You do me good, Edna. What is it about you that always makes me feel better for having been with you?"
>
> "My motherly presence; surely you've noticed. My comfortable shape, my lack of sexual competition, my reasonableness. As well as the fact that I'm very smart."
>
> "I deny I have ever sought or appreciated motherliness."
>
> "That's because you think of motherliness as like your own mother, or the mothers of your childhood friends. There is something all women like in an older, intelligent, assuaging female creature, and don't let anyone tell you otherwise. Women don't know how to define that comfort, because they find it so rarely, and because the word *comfort* seems to imply mindlessness. . . . How many women older than you are there in your life, or have there ever been, who have real power, whose *minds* you respect, and who are capable of being loved?"

I was well into adulthood before I learned to ask Heilbrun's question myself. As a young woman I knew older women who did have minds I respected, a few of whom did have real power, and all of whom were capable of being loved. I failed to recognize their significance for my life, however, for two reasons. When I was young I focused on the interesting things my brothers did that were entirely closed to me. Later, as I began to prepare for my vocation, I was keenly aware of the lack of professional mentors who in my time and place necessarily would have been male. For years I more than missed having them: I grieved their absence. It was a loss that seemed as irreparable as a child's loss of a mother at a very young age.

It was a long time before I turned my search for mentors to women, and longer still before I looked back to the women present in my childhood. When I did, I began to discover mentors all around. Once I realized that every mentor in the *Odyssey* was really Athena after all, the possibilities began to multiply. "Our literature," says Rollo May, "is the richest source of the presentation of human beings' self-interpretation down through history." Elsewhere he adds: "The loneliness of mythlessness is the deepest and least assuagable of all." To be without myths is to be without stories. The stories we choose, however, must be complex and fertile.

A paradox to the ancient Greeks, Athena is a paradox also to us. She is the goddess who loves peace but will make war if she has to. Her eyes flash with anger at injustice, but she also honors the olive branch of reconciliation. Thoroughly at home in a man's world, she is a prime protector also of the traditional world of women. She is both strong and beautiful, a warrior and a weaver, a father figure and a mother figure. Athena is as complex, in short, as our human situation is complex. That is why she represents so rich a symbol for life of both individuals and cities.

In his introduction to Nikos Kazantzakis's modern sequel to

the *Odyssey*, Kimon Friar describes the complex and even contradictory character of Odysseus as one who was

> modest yet boastful, cunning yet straightforward, heavy-handed yet gentle, affectionate yet harsh, aristocratic yet public-spirited. . . . Only one of the twelve Olympian deities had a character equally complex—she who in Homer was Odysseus's constant companion and protector, and for whom the Athenians named their city as a tribute to both their involved temperaments: Athena.

We live in a messy world. It is a contingent world, where disasters happen and diseases descend and hopes are dashed and trust is betrayed. In short, we live in a world that breaks our hearts if we stay around long enough.

But a broken heart is never, ever the end of the story. Comfort hovers around us on wings of grace. We heal, our community gathers around us, and we continue to be creative.

We are changed by those we love who have left us because we were formed by them while they were here. When someone we love dies or leaves, we have to revisit in new ways the places they inhabited in our hearts. It is not so much that we take part of them into us as that, in their absence, we discover or cultivate a part of us we did not know was there. This does not compensate for their loss. The loss is still loss, but our creative healing becomes part of their legacy to us. Those who went before are still our mentors, still helping us become who we alone can be.

Understanding mentors in the classical sense enables us not only to keep moving into the unknown, but also to carry with us a past that is continually being revised. Each glimpse of a mystery by which we have been formed makes us curious about the others we have missed.

Our mentors, present and past, keep us moving along on the journey. We may be quiet and still at times—wise friends remind us of the importance of stillness in our lives—but our mentors do not permit us to stay stuck. They want us to grow, and to grow is to keep moving into the unknown. A journey into the unknown is scary, because it always contains the possibility of new birth. For journeys in the wilderness, we are always being born again.

"The world was given to us in motion," writes Sister William in one of the Corita Kent's splendid posters, "and the forces of natural evolution keep it in motion, and the love and hope of those who keep an eye on that motion, who call our attention to that motion, and who give it shape with joy and celebration are revolutionaries and creators in a true sense of those words." The love and hope sustained by the mentors around us help keep the world in motion.

We do not earn or merit our mentors. They are gifts, plain and simple. The gift they give us is ourselves. Our response to such gifts can only be gratitude, reciprocity, and hearts and minds open to others we meet along the way.

SOURCES

Ashton-Warner, Sylvia. *Teacher* (New York: Simon and Schuster, 1963). [59]

Barondess, Jeremiah A. "A Brief History of Mentoring," *Transactions of the American Clinical and Climatological Association* 106 (1995): 1–24. [105]

Bonhoeffer, Dietrich. "The Friend" in *Letters and Papers from Prison*, The Enlarged Edition, ed. Eberhard Bethge (London: SCM Press, 1971; New York: Macmillan Co., 1971), 388–91. [76]

Brewer, Mary Louise. "The Chaotic Worlds of Apuleius and Kafka," in *Franz Kafka: His Place in World Literature, Proceedings of the Comparative Literature Symposium*, vol. 4, ed. Wolodymyr T. Zyla (Lubbock: Texas Tech University Press, 1971), 35–49. [14]

Ciardi, John, trans. *The Divine Comedy: Dante Alighieri* (New York: Norton, 1970). [112–13]

Clay, Jenny Strauss. *The Wrath of Athena: Gods and Men in the Odyssey* (Princeton: Princeton University Press, 1983), 3. [132]

Danilova, Alexandra. Quotation from her autobiography, *Choura*, *New York Times* (August 17, 1997): H30. [64–65]

Felson, Nancy. *Regarding Penelope: From Character to Poetics* (Princeton: Princeton University Press, 1994), 3, 62. [35]

Friar, Kimon. Introduction to *The Odyssey: A Modern Sequel* by Nikos Kazantzakis (New York: Simon and Schuster, 1958) xxvi. [134–35]

Gaillard, Frye. "Fossils among the Oaks," *Progressive* (April 1983): 18. [93]

Gerron, Peggy Sue. "Streets of Lubbock," *Lubbock Magazine* (October, 1996): 38–39. [62]

Goldrosen, John. *The Buddy Holly Story* (New York, London, and Tokyo: Quick Fox, 1979) 13–16. [60]

Hall, Roberta M., and Bernice R. Sandler. "Academic Mentoring for Women Students and Faculty: A New Look at an Old Way to Get Ahead" (Project on the Status and Education of Women, Association of American Colleges, 1983). [106]

Heilbrun, Carolyn. "Unmet Friends," in *The Last Gift of Time: Life Beyond Sixty* (New York: Dial Press, 1997), 137, 138, 149. [82–83, 99–100]

———. (pseud. Amanda Cross). *A Trap for Fools* (New York: E. P. Dutton, 1989), 84–85. [133]

Hyde, Anne P. Quoted in "Success at Work and as a Woman" by Judy Klemerud, *New York Times* (January 26, 1981): B6. [108]

Hyde, Lewis. *The Gift: Imagination and the Erotic Life of Property* (New York: Vintage, 1979), 45–49. [129–130]

Kazantzakis, Helen. *Nikos Kazantzakis, a Biography Based on His Letters*, trans. Amy Mims (New York: Simon and Schuster, 1968), 548, 559–60. [65, 81–82]

Kazantzakis, Nikos. *The Saviors of God*, trans. Kimon Friar (New York: Simon and Schuster, 1960), 69, 71, 72. [41–42]

Kristeva, Julia. *The Stranger within Ourselves*, trans. Leon S. Roudiez (New York: Columbia University Press, 1991), 183–88. [121]

MacIntyre, Alasdair. *After Virtue* (Notre Dame: University of Notre Dame Press, 1981), 181–82. [99]

Maddux, Rachel. *The Green Kingdom* (New York: Simon and Schuster, 1957). [19, 23, 27, 28]

———. *Communication: The Autobiography of Rachel Maddux, and Her Novella, Turnip's Blood*, ed. Nancy A. Walker (Knoxville: University of Tennessee Press, 1991). [18–24, 25, 28]

———. "A Princess in Oz: On Writing, by Rachel Maddux," ed. and intro. by Nancy A. Walker, *Santa Barbara Review* 1, no.2 (fall/winter 1993): 64–79. [19, 126–27]

———. *A Walk in the Spring Rain.* (New York: Doubleday, 1966), 34–35. [15, 16, 28]

May, Rollo. *The Cry for Myth* (New York and London: W. W. Norton and Company, 1991), 159, 99, 153. [113, 134]

MENTTIUM Corporation promotional materials, including description of its MENTTIUM 100sm program. Individual sheets and corporate booklet (Chicago, 1998). [106–107]

Miller, Barbara Stoler, trans. *The Bhagavad-Gita: Krishna's Counsel in Time of War* (New York: Bantam Books, 1986). [127–28]

Morrison, Toni. "Rootedness: The Ancestor as Foundation," in *Black Women Writers (1950-1980): A Critical Evaluation* (Garden City: Anchor Books, 1984), 343–44. [39]

Norman, Philip. *Rave On: The Biography of Buddy Holly* (New York: Simon and Schuster, 1996), 73–74. [61]

Oates, Wayne. *Confessions of a Workaholic* (New York: World Publishing, 1971), 45–56, 83–109. [125–26]

Olivier, Laurence. *On Acting* (New York: Simon and Schuster, 1986), 31–32, 153. [63–64]

Palmer, Laura. *Shrapnel in the Heart: Letters and Remembrances from the Vietnam Veterans Memorial* (New York: Random House, 1987), xv. [36]

Palmer, Parker J. *The Company of Strangers: Christians and the Renewal of America's Public Life* (New York: Crossroad, 1983), 130. [122–23]

Price, Meredith. "Confessions of an Ex-Sorority Girl," *Versus* 32, no.4 (January 1998): 46. [107–108]

Quigley, Martin Peter. *Mr. Blood's Last Night: End of an Era in Journalism* (St. Louis: Sunrise Publishing Company, 1980), 113. [18]

Rorem, Ned. Interviewed in "A Lifetime of Living and Dying in Song," *New York Times* (January 20, 1998): B6. [56–57]

Roth, Philip. "The Conversion of the Jews," in *Goodbye, Columbus and Five Short Stories* (Boston: Houghton Mifflin Company, 1959), 139–58. [123]

Saar, Betye, and Lezley Saar. Interview, *New York Times* (August 17, 1997): H31. [66–67]

Schleicher, Edmund. "The Bootstrap Syndrome" (Privately circulated, 1997). Quoted by permission of the author. [115–116]

Sennett, Richard. *Authority* (New York: Alfred A. Knopf, 1980), 191. [111–112]

Siegfried, John. "Hooked on Teaching," *Vanderbilt Magazine* 79, no.3 (summer 1997): 9. [107]

Steere, Douglas V. *Work and Contemplation* (New York: Harper & Brothers, 1957), 14–15. [126]

Sulloway, Frank J. *Born to Rebel: Birth Order, Family Dynamics, and Creative Lives* (New York: Vintage, 1997). [35–36]

Ward, Ed. "Holly and Hamburgers: No Place but Lubbock," *Austin American-Statesman* (September 12, 1980): F1, F7. [61]

ACKNOWLEDGMENTS

I thank the following people who provided help along the way:

Julia Bloch, for conversations about the *Bhagavad-Gita*, and Melissa Bloch, for making the connection

Richard E. Brown, who discerned this book before I did and then stood by it and me

Thadious Davis, who gave me more Toni Morrison than I knew to hope for

Olympia Dukakis, for timely teaching about stage and page

Barbara Holmes, for finding "I'm Available to You" in record time

Jan Friesinger, for broadening the matrix

Phong Ngo, for teaching me the science of "Planting Iris"

Edmund Schleicher, for his continuing contributions to the world

Thomas Van Nortwick, for introducing me to Lewis Hyde's *The Gift*

My most excellent close-to-home editors, Ashley and Nina, for their gifts of judgment, one more time

Portions of the description of Rachel Maddux appeared earlier as a foreword to *Communication, the Autobiography of Rachel Maddux, and Her Novella, Turnip's Blood*, ed. with an intro. by Nancy A.

Walker (Knoxville: University of Tennessee Press, 1991), xiii–xix. The discussion of Buddy Holly appeared earlier as "A Scholar's Holly: A Classics Professor Reflects on Buddy Holly's Achievement," *Lubbock Magazine*, vol. 3.9 (September 1997): 38–39. Both are used by permission.

INDEX OF NAMES
AND SUBJECTS

INDEX OF PASSAGES
FROM THE ODYSSEY